D1312598

DECADES OF THE
20TH
CENTURY

1950s

ELDORADO INK

DECADES OF THE 20TH CENTURY

1900s

1910s

1920s

1930s

1940s

1950s

1960s

1970s

1980s

1990s

DECADES OF THE
20ᵀᴴ CENTURY

1950s

ELDORADO INK

Published by Eldorado Ink
2099 Lost Oak Trail
Prescott, AZ 86303
www.eldoradoink.com

Milan Bobek, Editor
Judith C. Callomon, Historical consultant
Samuel J. Patti, Consulting editor

Printed and bound in Slovenia

Publisher Cataloging Data
1950s / [Milan Bobek, editor].
        p. cm. -- (Decades of the 20th century)
      Includes index.
      Summary: This volume, arranged chronologically, presents
key events that have shaped the decade, from significant political
occurrences to details of daily life.
      ISBN 1-932904-05-0
      1. Nineteen fifties   2. History, Modern--20th century--
Chronology   3. History, Modern--20th century--Pictorial works
I. Bobek, Milan   II. Title: Nineteen fifties   III. Series
      909.82/5--dc22

Picture research and photography by Anne Hobart Lang and Rolf
Lang of AHL Archives. Additional research by Heritage Picture
Collection, London.

CONTENTS

THE NUCLEAR AGE

Postwar paranoia flavors the decade: Espionage, Cold War, and witch hunts preoccupy the military and political classes. Unfinished business in the East leads to war in Korea and there are uprisings in Africa and Cuba. The babies who "boomed" in the 1940s grow up into a new phenomenon known as a teenager. Rock and roll is born: Elvis Presley thrusts his pelvis into the face of the Establishment and the Beat Generation try to articulate the joys of existential freedom. The space race begins with the U.S.S.R. launching the satellite *Sputnik*.

BACKGROUND: The handwriting of Albert Einstein, describing his theory of relativity.

1950–1959

KEY EVENTS OF THE DECADE

- KOREAN WAR
- COMMUNIST WITCH HUNTS
- CHINA INVADES TIBET
- ROCK AND ROLL
- CIVIL WAR IN CUBA
- MT. EVEREST CLIMBED
- DNA STRUCTURE DISCOVERED
- HYDROGEN BOMB
- BEAT
- THE WARSAW PACT

- POLIO VACCINE DEVELOPED
- HUNGARIAN UPRISING
- SUEZ CRISIS
- EEC SET UP
- RUSSIAN SPUTNIK IN SPACE
- CND FOUNDED
- ELVIS PRESLEY
- CASTRO TAKES CUBA

WORLD POPULATION 2,516 MILLION

...lls — wie dieselbe gegenwä[rtig]

...ihrer Anwendung auf bewegte

...elche den Phänomenen nicht

...t. Man denke z. B. an die elektr[o]

...schen einem Magneten und

...rnen hängt hier nur ab von

...n Magnet, während nach

...tälle, dass der eine oder der

...sei, streng voneinander zu

...iele der Magnet und ruht der

...des Magneten ein elektrisches

...nelches an den Orten, wo sich

...erzeugt. Ruht aber der Magnet

...et in der Umgebung des Magnet

...leiter eine elektromotorische

...ie entspricht, die aber — Gleichheit

...ins Auge gefassten Fällen ver[e]

WAR AND WITCH HUNTS

The Korean War breaks out when Communist North Korea invades South Korea. U.N. forces, headed by the United States, side with South Korea. Later in the year, China invades Tibet. The fight against Communism in the Western world becomes an obsession with a witch hunt in the United States and a spate of notorious spy trials. European countries make plans for a common trading market and television begins to play a major role in family life.

1 9 5 0

Feb	9	U.S. Senator McCarthy alleges that 205 Communists are working in the U.S. State Department
Mar	1	Atomic scientist Klaus Fuchs is sentenced to 14 years imprisonment for betraying secrets to the U.S.S.R.
May	1	Marriage Law passed in China gives women full equality in marriage and divorce
	9	Schuman Plan is proposed to create a single European authority for German and French coal production
June	25	North Korean forces invade Republic of South Korea Korean War breaks out
	28	North Korean forces capture Seoul, South Korea

July	1	First U.N. forces, comprised mostly from the United States, arrive in Korea
	31	King Leopold III of Belgium abdicates.
Sep	11	South African statesman Jan Smuts dies
	16	U.S. marines make amphibious landings at Inchon, Korea
	26	U.N. forces recapture Seoul, South Korea
Oct	1	South Korean and U.N. troops cross the 38th parallel which is the border between North and South Korea
	21	Chinese forces occupy Tibet
	23	Singer Al Jolson dies at age 67
Nov	24	U.N. forces launch offensive into North Korea
	26	Chinese forces enter Korean War

COMMUNIST WITCH HUNT

U.S. Senator Joe McCarthy (1909–1957) alleges that 57 Communists and 205 Communist sympathizers are working in the State Department. The Senate Foreign Relations Committee is given the job of investigating the charges, beginning an anti-Communist witch hunt in the United States. It lasts with McCarthy in charge until he attacks the U.S. Army in October 1953, leading to his censure in October 1954 and a rapid downfall.

SPY FEVER

In Britain, atomic scientist Dr Klaus Fuchs (1911–88) is arrested and jailed for 14 years for giving nuclear secrets to the Russians. The information he passed on enables Soviet scientists to advance their nuclear plans by many years. The following year, American Communists Julius and Ethel Rosenberg are tried and executed in the United States for similar crimes. In June 1951, two British diplomats, Guy Burgess and Donald MacLean, defect to the U.S.S.R. These and other cases lead to a spate of spy fever in the Western world.

COMMON ECONOMIC POLICY

French foreign minister Robert Schuman (1886–1963) puts forward a plan for pooling the French and German coal and steel industries under a joint authority, which other nations might join. The plan, worked out by French economist Jean Monnet, leads to the formation of the European Coal and Steel Community (ECSC). It is formed in Paris in April 1951 and joined by France, West Germany, Italy, and the Benelux countries. The ECSC starts functioning in July 1952.

PHILIPPINES HUK REBELLION

The Hukbalahap or People's Anti-Japanese Army, a Communist resistance group in Luzon, which has adopted guerrilla tactics against the newly independent Republic of the Philippines, attacks Manila. However, its secret headquarters in the capital is raided and the attack is called off. With U.S. military help and a program of reforms initiated by President Magsaysay, the popularity of the Huks wanes and the surviving leader surrenders in 1954.

MILLIONS WATCH TELEVISION

More than 75 million people watch the first transcontinental American television broadcast, marking the growing popularity of commercial network services since 1946. Color broadcasts are now transmitted by CBS. In the U.K., almost half a million television sets now tune into one BBC channel.

FOURTH WORLD CUP

The winner of the fourth soccer World Cup, hosted by Brazil, is decided by matches in a final pool of four teams. Uruguay wins for the second time but the pool system is never used again. England, the nation which invented the game, plays in the World Cup for the first time, but is beaten 1–0 by the United States.

ABOVE: Television becomes one of the most sought-after consumer products in the early 1950s.

ABOVE: The Dalai Lama is forced into exile and flees to Dharamsala in Punjab, India, where he is to set up an alternative government.

ABOVE: Motion pictures enter a new golden age in the early 1950s. *All The King's Men*, based on a Pulitzer Prize winning novel by Robert Penn Warren, stars Broderick Crawford, Jeanne Dru, John Ireland, John Derek, and Mercedes McCambridge.

UNIVERSITY CITY
Modernist architects Mario Pani and Enrique del Moral design this Central American complex, the campus of the Autonomous National University of Mexico.

HOW BIG IS PLUTO?
In March, Dutch-born U.S. astronomer Gerard P. Kuiper measures the planet Pluto and finds it is tiny. Its diameter is finally determined by the Hubble Space Telescope in the late 1990s to be 1,453 miles.

THE OORT CLOUD
Dutch astrophysicist Jan Oort (1900–92) suggests that there is a huge reservoir of comets at a great distance from the Sun; it is later known as the Oort Cloud.

ENTER CYCLAMATES
Cyclamates, artificial sweeteners much used in food and drinks as an alternative to saccharin, are introduced; some countries ban them.

KURT WEILL
(1900–1950)

German-born American composer Kurt Weill has died. The composer of "Mack the Knife" and "September Song" worked with Bertolt Brecht on *The Rise and Fall of the City of Mahagonny* (1927–1929) and the outstandingly successful *The Threepenny Opera* (1928). He left Nazi Germany in 1933 with his wife, the singer Lotte Lenya, and settled in the United States in 1935, where he composed several Broadway musicals.

JAN CHRISTIAN SMUTS
(1870–1950)

South African elder statesman and former prime minister Jan Christian Smuts has died. He helped to create the Union of South Africa (1910), was a member of the Imperial War Cabinet during World War l, and acted as counsel to the British War Cabinet during World War ll.

CHINESE WOMEN EQUAL
Mao Zedong's Communist government passes a new marriage law, which recognizes the role women played in the Communist victory. Chinese women now have full legal equality in marriage, divorce, and the ownership of property. Forced and arranged marriages, polygamy, child marriage, and infanticide are forbidden.

INSIDE THE CELL
Using an electron microscope, Belgian cytologist (cell specialist) Albert Claude (1899–1983) discovers the endoplasmic reticulum, a network of space inside a living cell that holds things together.

DINERS CREDIT CARD
Diners Club is founded by Ralph Schneider, who issues the first charge card, a prototype credit card (it is paid off every month). Two hundred cardholders pay an annual fee for credit at 27 New York restaurants.

VASLAV NIJINSKY
(1890–1950)

The great Russian dancer and choreographer Vaslav Nijinsky has died. Trained at the Imperial Ballet School at St. Petersburg, he became the leading dancer with Diaghilev's Ballets Russes. Sadly, after a period of internment in World War 1, he was diagnosed schizophrenic in 1917 and his life has been a struggle.

THE PLASTIC AGE

ABOVE: Newly invented nylon zippers are light enough for sheer fabrics and resistant to cleaning compounds.

ABOVE: A tough, moisture-resistant plastic called Tenite covers this portable radio case.

ABOVE: A clock encased in transparent plastic, a popular ornament.

RIGHT: A telephone handset made of Bakelite, an early plastic.

ABOVE: Plastics are easily molded and can be used to make intricate shapes such as this record rack.

KOREAN WAR

North Korean forces invade South Korea, leading to three years of bitter conflict. United Nations troops, led by the United States, aid South Korea, while China joins in on the North Korean side in November. North Korean forces push South Korean and U.S. forces down to a small perimeter at Pusan. In September 1950, U.S. marines land at Inchon, the port serving Seoul, the South Korean capital, as part of the U.N. breakout operation from Pusan. The landings, which are a success, lead to a counteroffensive up to the Chinese border. With a combined strength of 485,000, Chinese and North Korean troops drive the 365,000-strong United Nations forces south. A U.N. counterattack stabilizes the line. By June 1951, the two sides face each other across the 38th parallel. Negotiations and prisoner exchanges take place in 1953. By the end of the war, U.N. casualties are 118,515 killed, 264,591 wounded, and 92,987 captured. The Communist armies suffer 1,600,00 battle casualties, with 171,000 taken prisoner.

The Korean War sees the inaugural jet-versus-jet victory when in November 1950, an American U.S.A.F. F-80C shoots down a Chinese MiG-15 fighter over Sinuij on the Yalu River.

ABOVE: U.S. marines use scaling ladders to storm ashore during the amphibious landings at Inchon.

RIGHT:
A Korean
delegate to
Kaesong
Conference

ABOVE: Bombardment of warehouses in Wonsan.

ABOVE: A U.S. soldier comforts a fellow infantryman, while another
writes casualty tags.

ABOVE: United Nations troops fighting in the streets of Seoul.

ABOVE: A 75mm recoilless rifle is fired in support of infantry units near Oetlook-tong.

ABOVE: U.S. Marines advancing under close air support.

ABOVE: U.S. Navy Sky Raiders fire rockets at North Korean positions.

ABOVE: A soldier stands guard in a machine gun nest.

GENERAL DOUGLAS MACARTHUR

In July of 1950, President Truman received a request from the U.N. Security Council to designate a senior general to command all of the U.N. forces during the Korean campaign. He quickly appointed General Douglas MacArthur to the position. Their relationship was tumultuous from the onset. The general made no secret of his differences with the President. He criticized Truman's policy on Formosa, for failing to bomb Korean bases inside China, and attacked his policy of fighting a limited war in Korea. His actions led Truman to relieve him of his duties on April 11, 1951.

ABOVE: the USS *Missouri* fires a 16 inch salvo to disrupt communications in the north of the peninsula

CHINESE INVADE TIBET

The Chinese invade Tibet and although the Tibetans appeal to the U.N., their country is quickly overrun. The youthful Dalai Lama remains as a figurehead but finally escapes to India.

LEOPOLD ABDICATES

King Leopold III returns to Belgium after six years of exile and abdicates in favor of his son, Baudouin.

2,000 YEAR OLD DEATH

Tollund Man, a 2,000 year old corpse, is found preserved in a bog near Jutland, Denmark. Aged between 30 and 40, the man was killed by hanging or strangling and a leather rope is still around his neck.

STONE AGE NORTH POLE

The Danes complete a three year expedition to Greenland in which they find traces of a Stone Age culture 470 miles from the North Pole.

PACKAGE HOLIDAYS

Package holidays are launched by European entrepreneurs Gerard Blitz and Vladimir Raitz, who advertise inexpensive campsite accommodation in "holiday villages" on the islands of Majorca and Corsica.

FIRST JET AIRLINER SERVICE

The first jet airliner service is inaugurated with a flight from London to Paris in the Vickers Viscount 630 four-engined turboprop aircraft.

YOUTH FASHION

Bobbysoxers, so called because of the ankle-length socks they wear, emerge as a new youth group in the United States. They are teenage girl fans of the new singing sensation Frank Sinatra (1915–1998) and they follow him wherever he performs.

RASHOMON

Japanese director Akira Kurosawa's film *Rashomon* is premiered, establishing his worldwide reputation. It is a study of a violent crime from four different points of view. Kurosawa will later become famous for the epic Samurai movie *The Seven Samurai* (1954).

COMPUTER CHESS

U.S. mathematician Claude E. Shannon designs the first chess-playing computer.

TRUMAN ASSASSINATION ATTEMPT

Two Puerto Rican Nationalists fail in their attempt to kill President Truman at Blair House in Washington, D.C. where the president is residing.

SPIES, PACTS, AND BEATNIKS

War continues in Korea and French Indochina. Libya gains independence. A new and most advanced digital computer, the UNIVAC 1, is developed. It uses magnetic tape to input and output information and will have a revolutionary impact on business. American author J.D. Salinger's novel *The Catcher in the Rye* creates a hero whose alienation is understood by adolescents everywhere. Italian-American composer Menotti creates an opera specifically for television.

1951

Jan	1	North Koreans and Chinese take Seoul
	26	U.N. launches counteroffensive against Chinese and Korean forces
Mar	30	Julius and Ethel Rosenberg are found guilty of espionage
Apr	22	Battle of Imjin River, Korea. The U.N. takes defensive action against Chinese and Korean troops
May	25	British diplomats Burgess and Maclean are warned they are under suspicion of spying and leave Britain
Sep	1	United States, Australia, and New Zealand sign Pacific Security Agreement.
	8	Peace treaty signed with Japan
Dec	13	French National Assembly ratifies Schuman Plan
	24	Libya becomes independent

ABOVE: President Harry S. Truman addresses the American people. Television broadcasts are a common feature of the time.

OPPOSITE: Dramatic changes in aircraft design are represented by the 1912 "pusher" biplane, which can fly at 60 miles per hour, and the North American F-86 Sabre jet, which holds the world speed record of 670 miles per hour in 1951.

ABOVE: In Saudi Arabia, American experts advise on the use of scientific farming techniques to help grow crops, such as watermelons, in the desert soil.

PEACE AT LAST
Representatives of 49 nations meet in San Francisco and sign the peace treaty with Japan, formally bringing World War II hostilities to an end.

LIBYA INDEPENDENT
The former Italian colony of Libya becomes independent. Occupied by the British during the war, Libya becomes the first independent state created by resolution of the U.N. and the first former European colony in North Africa to gain independence.

FRENCH INDOCHINESE WAR
War continues in Indochina. The Vietminh establish a common front with Communist groups in Laos and Cambodia and move to conventional tactics.

PEST CONTROL
Biological pest control is tested in Australia. Myxomatosis is now being used by sheep farmers to kill rabbits. The rabbits were introduced by settlers in 1859 and now number over 500 million. They are rapidly consuming the grazing areas. In the United States, entomologist Edward F. Knipling of the Department of Agriculture introduces sterilization of female insects, which die without reproducing.

ABOVE: South Korean refugees, fleeing from fighting in their home area, follow a railroad track to what they hope will be a safer place.

THE CATCHER IN THE RYE
American writer J.D. Salinger (b. 1919) publishes a short novel, *The Catcher in the Rye*. It portrays the adolescent Holden Caulfield, who runs away from boarding school. Holden's attacks on the "phony" nature of adult attitudes make the novel an instant hit with teenagers.

TWO TERM LIMIT
The 22nd Amendment is passed prohibiting any president from being elected for more than two terms or more than one term if they have already served more than two years of the predecessor's term. It was passed in an attempt to limit presidential power.

AMAHL AND THE NIGHT VISITORS
U.S. composer Gian Carlo Menotti composes this work specifically for the increasingly popular medium of television. A Christmas work, it is premiered on Christmas Eve and is his most famous work.

BILLY BUDD
The opera *Billy Budd*, by English composer Benjamin Britten (1913–1976), is performed. It is based on Herman Melville's novel *Billy Budd*. Novelist E.M. Forster collaborates with Eric Crozier on the libretto and English tenor Peter Pears creates the lead role.

UNIVAC I ARRIVES
The first mass produced computer goes into production, the UNIVAC 1 (Universal Automatic Computer). It is the first computer to store its data on magnetic tape.

STICKY SUBJECT
U.S. scientist Fred Joyner accidentally discovers an adhesive that sticks to everything it touches. It turns out to be the first of the superglues, which harden in seconds in the absence of air.

FESTIVAL OF BRITAIN
The Festival of Britain opens in London around Robert Matthew's Royal Festival Hall and a Dome of Discovery. Exhibitions display new textiles, minimalist furniture of metal and plastic, and modern art and design. Telekinema, the star attraction, shows stereoscopic movies watched through polarizing spectacles.

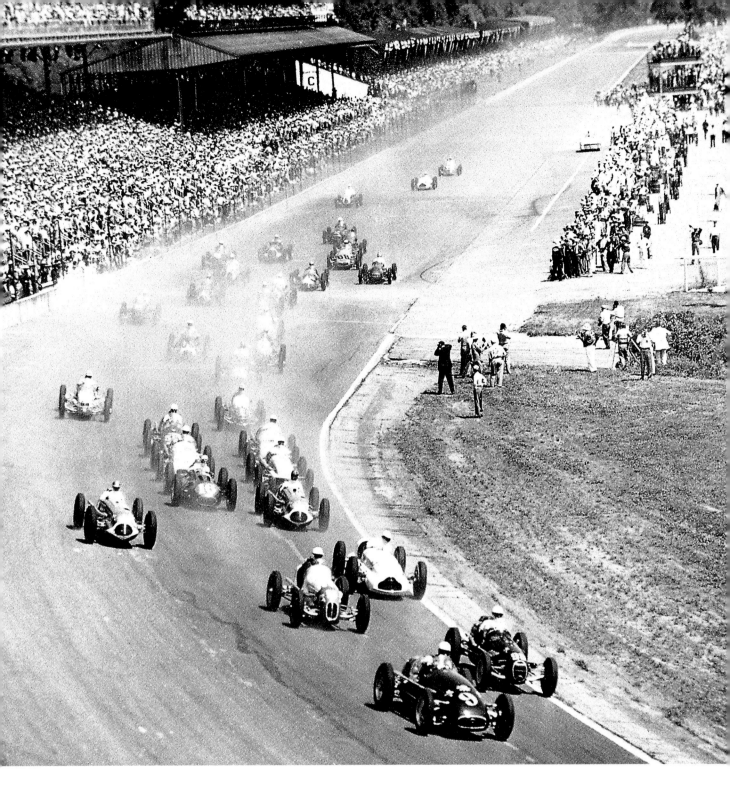

ABOVE: The 35th annual Memorial Day 500 mile race at Indianapolis, the Indy 500, is won by Lee Wallard. The winning time is a record of 3 hours 57 minutes and 38 seconds, at an average speed of 126.25 miles per hour. miles per hour.

THE MILKY WAY
U.S. astronomer William Morgan confirms that our own galaxy, the Milky Way, has a spiral structure; the solar system is on one arm of the spiral.

FLUORIDATION
Fluoride, naturally present in some drinking water, is discovered to prevent tooth decay. Authorities begin working to add fluoride to water supplies.

LUDWIG JOSEF JOHANN WITTGENSTEIN (1899–1951)

Austrian-born British philosopher Ludwig Wittgenstein has died of cancer in Cambridge. His early work, *Tractatus Logico-Philosophicus* (1921), was highly influential among contemporary philosophers. He immediately had a great personal following when, in 1945, he finally took up a post at Cambridge, although nothing further was published. His second major work, *Philosophical Investigations* (1953), and other writings will be published after his death.

ROCK AND ROLL IS HERE TO STAY

The United States tests an H-bomb in the Pacific Ocean as the U.S. and Soviet Union rivalry steps up. Mau Mau disturbances break out in Kenya against British colonial rule and a state of emergency is declared. Transistors are applied to a variety of uses from telephones to radios, and rock and roll bursts onto the popular music scene. The Cold War rivalry is reflected at the Olympic Games. General Dwight Eisenhower becomes President Eisenhower. Jonas Salk tests his vaccine against polio.

1952

Feb	6	The British king George VI dies and Queen Elizabeth II succeeds him
	14	Winter Olympics open in Oslo, Norway
	27	A treaty is signed with Japan that permits U.S. military bases on Japanese soil
Mar	1	India holds first national elections. Pandit Nehru's Congress Party wins 364 out of 489 seats in the National Assembly
July	19	Olympic Games open in Finland
	21	Massive earthquake hits California killing 11 people,
	25	Puerto Rico is given self-rule and becomes first U.S. Commonwealth
	26	Eva ("Evita") Perón dies of cancer
Sep	15	Eritrea is federated with Ethiopia, East Africa
Oct	7	The New York Yankees defeat the Brooklyn Dodgers at Ebbets Field to win the World Series
	20	Mau Mau disturbances begin. A state of emergency is declared in Kenya
Nov	1	U.S. scientists test a hydrogen bomb in the South Pacific
	4	Democrat John F. Kennedy defeats Republican incumbent Henry Cabot Lodge for the Massachusetts Senate seat
	5	Dwight D. Eisenhower wins the U.S. presidential election in a landslide victory over Adlai E. Stevenson
	9	Chaim Weizmann, first Israeli president, dies at the age of 77
Dec	10	Albert Schweitzer is awarded the Nobel Peace Prize
	17	President-elect Eisenhower visits Korea to assess the situation

ABOVE: The California wine districts of Napa, Sonoma, and Mendocino produce fine varieties of New World wines.

U.S. TESTS H-BOMB

American scientists test a hydrogen bomb at Eniwetk Atoll in the Marshall Islands of the Pacific. According to observers, a small island is completely obliterated in the blast. Radioactive dust rises some 25 miles high and spreads over 100 miles. The hydrogen bomb is a thermonuclear weapon, which works by nuclear fission.

"IKE" WINS PRESIDENTIAL ELECTION

In November, former U.S. General Dwight D. Eisenhower (1890–1969) wins the presidential election for the Republicans with a landslide over his Democratic opponent, Adlai Stevenson. His vice president is Richard Nixon.

MAU MAU CAMPAIGN

A revolt against British colonial rule in Kenya breaks out, headed largely by the Kikuyu and Meru tribes. The British declare a state of emergency and commit 50,000 troops. Trouble continues until 1960.

NEW BRITISH QUEEN

George VI dies and Princess Elizabeth (b. 1926) becomes queen as Elizabeth II. Many heads of state attend the state funeral in London.

ERITREA FEDERATED WITH ETHIOPIA

In East Africa, the former Italian colony Eritrea is federated by the U.N. with Ethiopia.

DEATH OF EVITA

Eva Perón (Evita), much-loved and popular wife of President Juan Perón, dies from cancer. Her death starts the gradual erosion of his appeal.

ROCK AND ROLL ARRIVES

In the United States, rock and roll is launched with Alan Freed's Moondog's Rock'n'Roll Party on the WJW radio station in Cleveland, Ohio. The teen style movement has also reached the U.K., where Teddy boys dress in updated Edwardian fashions.

THE COMET FLIES

The world's first all-jet airliner, Britain's De Havilland DH 106 Comet 1, inaugurates a regular passenger service between London and Johannesburg.

ELEMENTS DISCOVERED

Elements 99 and 100, einsteinium and fermium, are discovered after a hydrogen bomb explosion by U.S. scientists working at the University of California and two national laboratories.

WAITING FOR GODOT

Irish writer Samuel Beckett's most famous play, *Waiting for Godot*, is performed and becomes a theatrical landmark. It portrays two tramps who wait for the mysterious Godot, who never comes. Their predicament seems to reflect the hopelessness of the modern world.

UNITE D'HABITATION

French architect Le Corbusier (1887–1965) creates a remarkable housing development in Marseilles. It incorporates facilities such as shops, a swimming pool, a gym, and a childcare center, as well as apartments. It meets the architect's aim of housing an entire community in a vast modernist block.

MULTIPLE-USE TRANSISTORS

In Japan, the first pocket-sized transistor radio is produced by Masaru Ibuka. He improves the technology designed by the Western Electric Co. division of AT&T and launches it under the Sony name. The first transistorized hearing aids are produced in the United States. In the U.K., transistors are applied to central telephone dialing apparatus to provide automatic dialing.

WRECK INVESTIGATION BY SCUBA

The first archaeological investigation of a wreck using scuba diving equipment is carried out by French diver and marine archaeologist Jacques Cousteau. He discovers an ancient Greek ship off the coast of Marseilles which contains wine urns.

ANTABUSE

Antabuse™, a drug which helps alcoholics to stop drinking, is introduced; its generic name is disulphiram.

GAS CHROMATOGRAPHY

British biochemists Archer Martin and A.T. James invent gas chromatography, a method of separating chemical vapors.

4'33"

American composer John Cage (1912–1992) has "written" a piano piece containing 4 minutes and 33 seconds of silence. The audience is encouraged to listen to the noises in the environment around them.

DREAMING SLEEP

Biologists studying sleep patterns discover a period in which a sleeper's eyes move rapidly. It is known as dreaming sleep or rapid eye movement (REM) sleep.

INSULIN ANALYZED

British biochemist Frederick Sanger (b. 1918) discovers that insulin is a protein and works out its structure.

MARIA MONTESSORI
(1870–1952)

Italian educational pioneer and physician Maria Montessori has died. Her teaching methods, which include learning through play, were developed from her early experiences in her school for children with learning disabilities. Montessori schools have become established as a leading method of teaching nursery and primary school children throughout the world.

CHAIM AZRIEL WEIZMANN
(1874–1952)

Israel's first president, Dr. Chaim Weizmann, has died. An eminent chemist of Russian birth, as a young man he worked in Switzerland where he became a leading Zionist. In Great Britain, where he lived from 1904 until 1934, he discovered the bacterium *Clostridium acetobutylium*, which is active in producing acetone from carbohydrate.

RIGHT: Television studios boom in response to the huge popularity of the new medium.

FLOAT GLASS

English glassmaker Arthur Pilkington invents float glass, in which liquid glass is floated on a bath of molten tin, producing a completely flat and shiny sheet.

AMNIOCENTESIS

Doctors develop amniocentesis, a procedure during pregnancy by which some of the amniotic fluid in a woman's womb can be examined to see if the baby she is carrying is healthy; it is used only in high-risk cases.

ACRYLIC GOES ON THE MARKET

New acrylic fibers such as Orlon, discovered by Du Pont, and Acrilan, produced by the Chemstrand Corporation, are marketed in the United States. They are soft and when spun into yarn they can be knitted like wool.

ANTARCTIC MAPPED

The Antarctic is mapped by air and major glaciers are explored by a Norwegian, Swedish, and British expedition. It is organized by H.V. Sverdrup, former director of the Scripps Institution and professor of Oceanography at the University of California.

AUSTRALIAN DISCOVERS ORE MOUNTAIN

An iron ore mountain is discovered in the Hammersley Range by Australian prospector Langley Hancock, who spots rust-colored outcroppings when his aircraft is blown off course. He keeps it secret, awaiting a change in mining laws before staking his claim.

FIRST SUGARLESS SOFT DRINK

No-Cal Ginger Ale, the first sugar-free soft drink, uses the new cyclamate sweeteners instead of sugar. It is also salt-free, so it is suitable for people with obesity, diabetes, and high blood pressure.

SCANDINAVIAN OLYMPICS

Mammoth crowds in Oslo, Norway, welcome the Winter Olympics to Scandinavia for the first time. Spectators on skis encourage cross-country competitors. 150,000 fans set an Olympic record to watch the ski jumping, and home cheers ring out for speed skater Hjalmar "Hjallis" Andersen's three gold medals. Athletes from the U.S.S.R. take part for the first time in the Summer Olympics held in Helsinki. Emil Zatopek (b. 1922), the "Czech Express," thrills Finnish spectators and takes golds in the 5,000m, 10,000m, and the marathon.

MARIA EVA (EVITA) DUARTE DE PERON (1919–1952)

Eva Perón, the immensely popular second wife of the Argentine populist right-wing president Juan Perón, has died from cancer at the age of 33. She had a strong influence on her husband and pursued the cause of women's suffrage and social and healthcare reform. Her death is greatly mourned by the Argentine people.

DOUBLE HELIX DECODED

Soviet ruler Joseph Stalin dies and is succeeded by Nikita Khrushchev. The Korean War comes to an end. British scientists begin to unlock life's secrets by discovering the structure of DNA and the world's highest mountain, Mt. Everest, is finally climbed. An American conservationist warns of the dangers of misusing the Earth's natural resources, and the "golden arches" are debuted in Phoenix, Arizona.

1953

Jan	**20**	Dwight D. Eisenhower is inaugurated as the 34th President of the United States and millions view the first ever nationwide broadcast
Feb	**10**	Common market for coal and steel begins among various European nations
Mar	**5**	Joseph Stalin, leader of the Soviet Union, dies at the age of 73
Apr	**25**	British scientists discover the structure of DNA
May	**29**	Mountaineers Hillary and Tensing reach the peak of Mt. Everest; the news is received on June 1
June	**17**	Worker's strike turns into an uprising against the Communist government in East Berlin
June	**19**	Julius and Ethel Rosenberg are executed in the electric chair for selling atomic secrets to the Soviets
July	**5**	Imre Nagy becomes prime minister of Hungary
	26	Fidel Castro leads an attempt to overthrow the Batista government in Cuba
	27	Armistice is signed ending the Korean War. Tensions still remain as South Korea refused to participate in the ceremony
Sep	**12**	Nikita Khrushchev is appointed the first secretary of the Central Committee of the Communist Party in the Soviet Union
Oct	**5**	The New York Yankees defeat the Dodgers to win a record fifth consecutive World Series

STALIN DIES
Joseph Stalin, leader of the U.S.S.R. for nearly 30 years, dies at the age of 73. He is succeeded by Georgi Malenkov as prime minister. In September, Nikita Khrushchev (1894–1971) becomes Communist party first secretary.

KOREAN WAR ENDS
An armistice is signed in Panmunjon, Korea, bringing to an end the three year old Korean War. Prisoners are exchanged and both sides withdraw from occupied areas. Under the agreement, Korea remains divided into North and South Korea.

UPRISING CRUSHED
In East Berlin, a worker's uprising against the partition of the city and the harsh Soviet rule is put down by Soviet tanks.

REGIME RELAXES IN HUNGARY
Imre Nagy (1895–1958) becomes the new prime minister of Hungary. He announces an end to enforced collectivization of agriculture and begins to relax Communist rule.

SHELLFISH POISONING
Environmental poisoning is identified as the cause of deaths from eating fish and shellfish caught in Minamata Bay in Kyushu and Niigata in Honshu, Japan. The waters are found to be contaminated with lead, a byproduct of industrial processes.

ABOVE: Czech refugees make a dramatic escape to the West by crashing through the Czech-German border in a stolen tank.

BELOW: After the armistice is signed in July 1953, peace negotiations to end the Korean War continue and prisoner exchanges are completed in September.

ABOVE: A miniature weapon used by East German secret agents in the continuing conflict with the West. It is a standard cigarette case concealing cyanide-coated bullets.

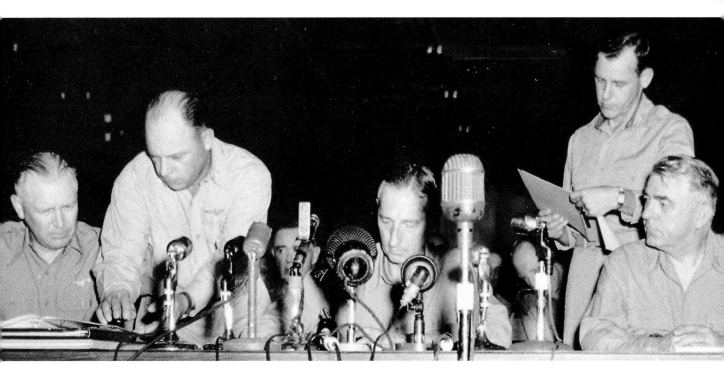

ABOVE: East Germans burn and trample Soviet flags during riots in the divided city of Berlin.

CUBAN CIVIL WAR

Communist rebel leader Fidel Castro (b. 1927) leads an attack on army barracks in Cuba in an unsuccessful attempt to overthrow Cuban premier Batista. Some rebels are killed and Castro is imprisoned.

COMMON COAL AND STEEL

The countries involved in the European Coal and Steel Community, France, Italy, Luxembourg, Belgium, the Netherlands, and West Germany, begin operating a common market for coal, iron ore, and steel.

BACKGROUND: Atomic bomb tests are conducted at Bikini Atoll in the Pacific Ocean.

DOUBLE HELIX

British scientists Francis Crick, James Watson, Maurice Wilkins, and Rosalind Franklin discover the structure of the complex molecule DNA (deoxyribonucleic acid), the chemical that forms the basis of genes which pass on hereditary characteristics. The structure of DNA is made up of two strands that intertwine to form a double helix. With this discovery, scientists can now establish how living things reproduce themselves.

NETHERLANDS FLOODS

Hurricane winds and abnormally high tides cause heavy flooding in the Netherlands and hundreds of people are drowned. Work immediately begins on the 30 year Delta Project to build dams across coastal estuaries and inlets. It will include a pioneering storm surge barrier across the Oosterschelde Estuary and the world's longest bridge across the Scheldt River.

UNDER MILK WOOD

Welsh poet Dylan Thomas (1914–1953) puts his vivid language and humor to use to create a play for voices. *Under Milk Wood* is set in a Welsh seaside town and deals with the daily lives, loves, and dreams of the inhabitants. Thomas takes a lead role in the play, which is performed in New York City, but dies later in the year.

EARTH'S LIMITS

American zoologist and conservationist Fairfield Osborne publishes *The Limits of Our Earth*. It warns of the consequences of misusing available natural resources and the dangers of overpopulation. In *Our Plundered Planet*, published in 1948, he had explained the dangers of using DDT.

THE CRUCIBLE

American playwright Arthur Miller's play *The Crucible* is performed. It takes as its subject the 17th century witchcraft trials in Salem, Massachusetts, using them as a metaphor for the McCarthyite hunting and trial of "communists" in contemporary America.

ABOVE: Methods for the disposing of nuclear waste include burying it deep underground.

HEART-LUNG MACHINE

U.S. surgeon John H. Gibbon develops a heart-lung machine and uses it to keep a patient alive while performing heart surgery.

GEODESIC DOME

Geodesic domes appear at Ford's headquarters in Dearborn, Michigan. They are the invention of designer and writer Richard Buckminster Fuller (1895–1983), who developed them in the 1930s and 1940s. Based on polyhedra, geodisic domes are designed to allow the maximum space to be covered with the most lightweight structure. They are also cheap to make and easy to prefabricate and assemble.

MICROWAVE OVEN

Percy L. Spencer, working for a firm in Massachusetts, patents the microwave oven. Used initially for commercial catering, it is later manufactured for domestic use.

EVEREST CONQUERED

New Zealander Edmund Hillary and Tibetan sherpa Tenzing Norgay, become the first climbers to reach the 29,039 foot summit of Mt. Everest, the world's highest mountain.

STRANGENESS

U.S. physicist Murray Gell-Mann introduces the term "strangeness" to classify subatomic particles.

RIGHT: Joseph Stalin, real name Iosif Vissarionovich Dzugashvili, dies. Expelled from a seminary in his youth for his Marxist evangelism, he rose through the ranks to lead the U.S.S.R.

MASER

U.S. physicist Charles Townes invents a device for generating high intensity microwaves; he calls it a maser, short for Microwave Amplification by Stimulated Emission of Radiation.

CREAM IN YOUR COFFEE?

Powdered cream for coffee, produced by M&R Dietetic Laboratories of Ohio in 1950, is followed by the production of dried milk by American dairy scientist David D. Peebles.

SCIENTOLOGY FOUNDED

The Church of Scientology is founded in Washington, D.C., by a former seaman, Lafayette Ronald Hubbard. His science of Dianetics is a form of psychotherapy designed to eliminate neuroses and offer a spiritual alternative to personal problems.

GO TELL IT ON THE MOUNTAIN

African American writer James Baldwin (1924–1987) publishes his first novel, *Go Tell it on the Mountain*. Set in Harlem, and based on his own life, it establishes him on the literary scene as a writer who will portray the lives and plights of black Americans.

SOCCER SHOCK

The Hungarian soccer team, captained by Ferenc Puskas, defeats the English team by 6–3 at the English home ground at Wembley. They become the first overseas team to defeat England at home.

DISPOSABLE BIC

The Bic, a disposable ballpoint pen devised by Baron Bich, is sold in Paris.

JOSEPH STALIN
(1879–1953)

The Soviet ruler, Joseph Stalin, has died. Born in Georgia, the son of a shoemaker, Stalin became a Bolshevik and in 1922 was appointed General Secretary to the Central Committee. He began to build a power base and, after Lenin died in 1924, succeeded him as leader of the Soviet Union, ruthlessly crushing all opposition to his leadership. Through collectivization and a series of five year plans, he transformed the Soviet economy and established it as a world power.

TROUBLE IN ALGERIA AND VIETNAM

Anti-French violence flares in Algeria as a war for independence begins. Vietnam, Laos, and Cambodia gain independence and Vietnam is divided into two. The arrival of the nuclear age is established by the launch of the world's first nuclear-powered submarine and the opening of the world's first nuclear reactor. An English athlete runs a mile in less than four minutes, Marlon Brando becomes a cult figure, and the world's first successful kidney transplant is performed.

1 9 5 4

Jan	21	First nuclear-powered submarine is launched in the United States
Mar	1	United States tests the hydrogen bomb in the Marshall Islands and causes widespread concern
Apr	9	Comet jet airliner crashes north of Messina, Sicily
	12	700 Mau Mau activists are arrested in Kenya
May	6	Roger Bannister breaks the four minute mile record
	7	French troops are forced to surrender in Dien Bien Phu, Vietnam
	17	U.S. Supreme Court rules that racial segregation in schools is unconstitutional
June	27	World's first nuclear power station opens in the U.S.S.R.
July	19	Boeing 707 makes its maiden flight from Seattle
	20	Armistice is signed in Geneva ending French Indochinese War. Cambodia, Laos, and Vietnam gain independence and Vietnam is divided along the 79th parallel
Sep	8	Southeast Asia Treaty Organization (SEATO) established
Oct	8	Communist forces occupy Hanoi, North Vietnam
Nov	1	Violence breaks out in Algeria. Algerian War of Independence begins
	3	French post-Impressionist Henri Matisse dies at the age of 84
Dec	2	U.S. Senate condemns Senator Joseph McCarthy

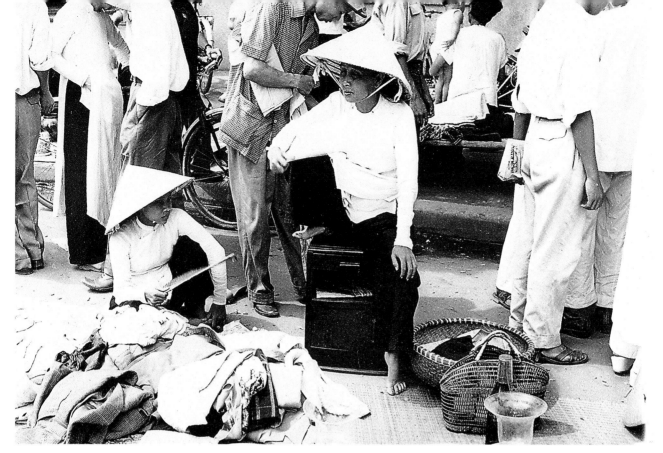

ABOVE: Vietnamese civilians in Hanoi set up informal street markets while waiting to be evacuated to the south.

VIETMINH TAKE DIEN BIEN PHU

In Vietnam, some 10,000 French troops are surrounded at Dien Bien Phu by the 50,000 member Vietminh Army led by General Giap. They are forced to surrender after a savage 56 day siege. This defeat leads to a series of agreements signed between France and other powers. France recognizes the independence of Cambodia and Laos and agrees to the independence and partition of Vietnam: the Communist-led north under Ho Chi Minh (1890–1969) and the pro-Western south, a republic under Ngo Dinh Diem (1901–1963).

ROCKING AROUND THE CLOCK

Bill Haley and the Comets release their latest record "Rock Around the Clock." It rapidly sells a million copies and within a year has become a youth anthem, establishing the new sound of rock and roll. In Memphis, Tennessee, Elvis Presley (1935–1977) records "That's All Right Momma" for Sun Records.

SEATO FORMED

Eight nations including, the United States, Australia, New Zealand, Pakistan, Thailand, the Philippines, Britain, and France, sign a defense treaty in Manila. It establishes the Southeast Asian Treaty Organization (SEATO) as a defense against Communist power in the region.

A MILE IN UNDER FOUR MINUTES

English athlete Roger Bannister achieves the holy grail of middle-distance running and runs a mile in under four minutes. Bannister, a 25 year old medical student, breaks the four minute barrier at the Oxford University running track, running the mile in 3 minutes and 59.4 seconds.

ABOVE: The French Foreign Legion questions a Vietminh soldier in the Indochinese War.

HENRI EMILE BENOIT MATISSE
(1869–1954)

The great French painter, stained glass artist, and sculptor Henri Matisse has died in his 80s. Even as an old man, he continued to work, most recently on making pictures from cutout paper (*L'Escargot*, 1953). As a young man, Matisse was one of the group known, from 1905, as the fauves (wild ones). Although he was influenced by cubism (and gave the movement its name), his painting was more representational. He has been admired for his flow of line and use of pure color.

SOLAR BATTERY
The solar battery is developed by Bell Laboratories of AT&T, making it possible to convert sunlight to electric power. The Association for Applied Solar Energy is founded and a periodical is launched, *The Sun at Work*.

BRANDO ON THE WATERFRONT
Starring Marlon Brando as an ex-prizefighter, *On the Waterfront* is the latest film directed by Elia Kazan. Brando's performance will gain him an Oscar and follows his powerful performance as a leather-clad motorbike gang leader in *The Wild One*.

DUTCH AUTONOMY FOR TERRITORIES
The Dutch government grants full domestic autonomy to its territories in South America and the West Indies.

NUCLEAR POWER PLANT
The first nuclear power plant to produce electricity is built in the Soviet Union, near Moscow. It is capable of generating 5 megawatts of electricity, enough for a small town.

ALGERIAN WAR OF INDEPENDENCE
An insurrection breaks out against French rule in the North African colony of Algeria, which France regards not as a colony, but rather as mainland France. The rebels call themselves the Algerian National Liberation Front (FLN) and launch what is to be a long and bloody struggle for independence that continues until 1962. The French win the military campaign but lose the political battle in the U.N. When General de Gaulle becomes president in 1958, he pulls out of Algeria.

ABOVE: Yugoslav troops parade in honor of the visit to Belgrade of President Bayar of Turkey to sign the tripartite alliance between Yugoslavia, Turkey, and Greece.

LIJNBAAN, ROTTERDAM

This long pedestrian shopping way, stretching some 656 yards from Rotterdam's commercial center to the railroad station, becomes highly influential in town planning. Many other pedestrian precincts will soon follow all over Europe.

TABLE TENNIS CHAMPIONS

The Table Tennis World Championships take place in London. China and Japan are confirmed as new powers in the sport when they displace previous leaders Hungary and Czechoslovakia.

SUCCESSFUL KIDNEY TRANSPLANT

U.S. surgeons J. Hartwell Harrison and Joseph Murray carry out the first successful kidney transplant, the donor being the recipient's identical twin brother.

VTOL AIRCRAFT

The U.S. Navy's Convair XFY-1 fighter aircraft makes its first test flight; it is a VTOL (Vertical Take-Off and Landing) aircraft, nicknamed the "flying pogo stick."

FIRST NUCLEAR SUBMARINE

The world's first nuclear-powered submarine, the *Nautilus*, begins service with the U.S. Navy. It is powered by two steam turbines, with the heat for the steam being provided by a nuclear reactor.

LA STRADA

The poetic, tragicomic movie *La Strada* by Italian film director Federico Fellini (1920–1993) is premiered. It portrays the lives of two wandering mountebanks, stars Fellini's wife, Giulietta Masina, and has a memorable score by Nino Rota.

LORD OF THE FLIES

English novelist William Golding (1911–1993) publishes *Lord of the Flies*. The novel describes what happens when, after a plane crash on a desert island, a group of schoolboys try to create a democratic society. The social order rapidly degenerates and reverts to savagery.

PLASTIC LENSES

Contact lenses, known since 1887, are now available in plastic, and are lighter and more comfortable to wear.

SEGREGATION UNCONSTITUTIONAL

The U.S. Supreme Court rules in the Brown v. Board of Education case that racial segregation in schools is unconstitutional. The judgment leads to considerable racial tension throughout the southern states.

EATING IN FRONT OF THE TV

TV dinners, a new convenience food, are introduced in the United States by Omaha's C.A. Swanson & Sons.

ABOVE: An anti-Communist former prisoner of war jubilantly waves the South Korean flag on reaching Seoul.

ABOVE: The crashed remains of a Czech airplane flown across the Iron Curtain to West Germany by Karel Cihak.

ABOVE: The Dalai Lama and Chairman Mao Zedong welcome each other at the First National People's Congress in Beijing were Mao is re-elected to another four year term.

ABOVE: Pierre Mendes-France of France, Anthony Eden of Great Britain, and John Foster Dulles of the U. S., meet with Germany's Chancellor Konrad Adenauer in Paris to end postwar occupation.

JOE AND MARILYN
Former New York Yankee star Joe Dimaggio and actress Marilyn Monroe are married in San Francisco. The marriage will last less than one year when Monroe sues for divorce citing incompatible career demands.

GUNMEN ATTACK CONGRESS
Five Congressmen were shot, one injured seriously, when a group of four Puerto Rican extremists opened fire in the House of Representatives. The militants were subdued and placed under arrest.

TOSCANINI RETIRES
After 68 years at the podium, Arturo Toscanini retires at the age of 87. In his final appearance, he conducted the NBC Symphony Orchestra in a program dedicated to the works of Wagner.

COUP IN GUATEMALA
Following mounting pressures from a ten day military siege, Communist President Jacobo Arbenz announces his resignation. The military junta appoints Colonel Diaz as the country's new President.

BRAZILIAN PRESIDENT COMMITS SUICIDE
Facing increasing pressure to resign because of financial corruption in his administration, President Vargas commits suicide just hours after resigning.

HO CHI MINH RETURNS
After 8 years in hiding, Ho Chi Minh quietly returns to Hanoi in October and resumes his position as Communist leader. His arrival signals the end of more than 70 years of French dominance.

SENATOR MCCARTHY CONDEMNED
In response to Senator McCarthy's tactics used in the Senate during his investigation of Communists in the U.S. Government, the Senate votes to condemn him for conduct unbecoming a Senator. While he was not officially censured, the Senate's action will greatly reduce his influence and stature.

ENRICO FERMI
(1901–1954)

The eminent nuclear physicist Enrico Fermi has died. He was born in Italy during 1901, where he studied and worked until 1938. He and his colleagues were the first to split uranium atoms by bombarding them with neutrons, contributing to the development of nuclear power and nuclear weapons. He was awarded the Nobel Prize for Physics in 1938. He left for the United States and became a naturalized citizen, because of his dislike of Italian anti-Semitism. He was responsible for building the world's first nuclear reactor in Chicago in 1942.

MOONIES

The Unification Church is founded by Korean evangelist Reverend Sun Myung Moon. His acolytes are dubbed "Moonies." Moon becomes notorious for arranging mass marriages between members of the church who do not meet until the day of their wedding.

COMETS CRASH

Following yet another crash by a Comet airliner, this time north of Messina, Sicily, all Comets are grounded and one is tested to destruction. Metal fatigue in the cabin is found to be the cause of the disasters.

BIKINI ATOLL

The United States tests its second H-bomb at Bikini Atoll in the Marshall Islands. It is more than 500 times as powerful as the A-bomb dropped on Hiroshima and its effects cause considerable concern. Nearby Japanese fishermen suffer radiation burns and sickness.

GERMANY BEATS HUNGARY

The talented Hungarian soccer team is beaten by Germany in the final of the 1954 World Cup in Switzerland. Hungarian star player Ferenc Puskas scores a goal but the final score is 3–2 to Germany.

BIRTH PILL TESTED

The first oral contraceptive, a pill for women containing a synthetic hormone, is developed by U.S. physiologist Gregory Pincus. It is successfully tested in Puerto Rico the following year.

NASSER BACK IN POWER

Gamal Abdel Nasser has taken power once again in Egypt. President Mohammed Naguib was removed from office and placed under house arrest. Earlier in the year, Nasser was in power for 3 days. Nasser's authority has been increasing since his successful negotiations with the British over the Suez Canal.

ABOVE: Rocky Marciano delivers the winning punch that ends the challenge of Ezzard Charles.

AN END TO SEGREGATION

An amnesty in Kenya ends the Mau Mau rebellion. Countries in Africa and Asia join together to form a nonaligned bloc, separate from both superpowers. Eastern European nations form the Warsaw Pact as a counter to NATO. Polio vaccine goes on trial and a new vehicle, the hovercraft, is patented. The Beat Generation finds its voice. Jazzman Charlie Parker dies, as does the great scientist Albert Einstein. Rosa Parks refuses to take a back seat.

1955

Jan 18   Amnesty is declared in Kenya to calm the Mau Mau rebellion

Mar 12   U.S. jazzman Charlie Parker dies at the age of 34

Apr 5   British Prime Minister Winston Churchill resigns at the age of 80

     18   Afro-Asian Conference is held in Bandung, Indonesia, to form "nonaligned" bloc. It lasts until April 24

     18   German-born scientist Albert Einstein dies of a heart attack at the age of 76

May 14   Warsaw Pact is established and unifies the Eastern Bloc nations militarily

     15   Austria's independence is restored after 17 years of occupation

June 11   More than 80 spectators and one driver are killed during the Le Mans car race outside of Paris. Race track officials do not cancel the race

July 18   Disneyland theme park opens in Anaheim, California at the cost of $17,000,000

Aug 30   Greek, Turkish, and British foreign ministers meet in London to discuss Cyprus. The meeting lasts until September 7

Sep 30   U.S. film star James Dean dies in a car crash at the age of 23

Dec 5   The American Federation of Labor and the Congress of Industrial Organizations join forces under the leadership of George Meany

WARSAW PACT

In response to West Germany joining NATO in October 1954, seven Eastern European nations, Albania, Bulgaria, Czechoslovakia, East Germany, Hungary, Poland, and Romania, plus the U.S.S.R., establish the Warsaw Pact. This provides for a unified military structure with its headquarters in Moscow and the stationing of Soviet armed forces in member countries.

BLACK WOMAN ARRESTED

In Montgomery, Alabama, American civil rights campaigner Rosa Parks is arrested for sitting in the front of the bus in seats reserved for white people after the Interstate Commerce Commission orders the desegregation of transport. Her arrest leads to a mass boycott of all buses in Montgomery, led by Martin Luther King Jr. (1929–1968).

MENDELEVIUM

Element 101 is produced artificially by a U.S. team headed by Glenn T. Seaborg. It is named mendelevium.

NONALIGNED BLOC

Leaders of 29 African and Asian countries meet in Bandung, Indonesia, at the invitation of President Sukharno (1902–70). They form a nonaligned bloc of countries opposed to the "imperialism and colonialism" of the superpowers, the U.S. and the U.S.S.R.

THE FAMILY OF MAN

Photographer Edward Steichen (1879–1973) mounts a notable exhibition at New York's Museum of Modern Art. A showcase of photography, it contains just over 500 photographs selected from more than two million.

ABOVE: Berlin students hold torches in memory of the Germans who lost their lives in the uprising of June 17, 1953. BELOW: Prime Minister Nehru of India discusses policy with Vice President Richard Nixon on his visit to India.

BELOW: Rosa Parks is arrested for violating the segregation laws in Montgomery, Alabama.

ABOVE: Dizzy Gillespie, the originator of bebop jazz, hits a high note for New York Democrat Adam Clayton Powell, Jr.

HELP IN THE KITCHEN

French engineer Mark Grégoire begins producing and marketing nonstick frying pans coated with polytetrafluoroethylene (PTFE), a slippery plastic material discovered in 1938.

SYNTHETIC DIAMONDS

The General Electric Research Laboratory in the United States makes the first synthetic diamonds by treating carbon at very high temperature and pressure. The first products are small diamonds of industrial quality.

LOLITA

Russian-born U.S. novelist Vladimir Nabokov (1899–1977) publishes *Lolita*. A novel about the infatuation of a middle-aged writer with a young girl, it provokes a storm of controversy and increases Nabokov's reading audience.

KILLER SMOG

In the U.K., a new Clean Air Act attempts to control city air pollution by banning the burning of soft, smog-producing coal. Smog in London and other major British cities, as well as in the United States, has killed more than 9,000 people since 1950.

DISNEYLAND OPENS

U.S. film director Walt Disney (1901–1966) and creator of world-famous cartoon character Mickey Mouse, has opened a fantastic Disneyland amusement theme park at Anaheim, California. It features a whole host of rides and attractions based on the Disney cartoons.

LEFT: President Ngo Dinh Diem of South Vietnam, in discussion with Buddhist priests.

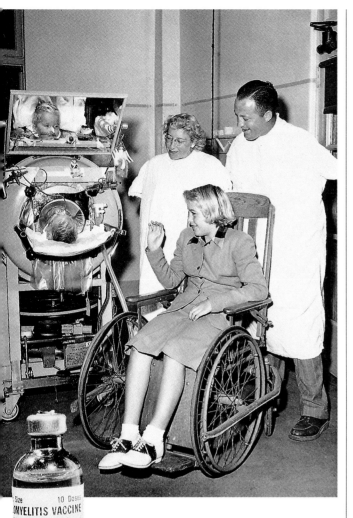

CYPRUS WAR OF INDEPENDENCE
Greek Cypriots begin a guerrilla war of independence against Britain. Their leading organization is the National Organization of Cypriot Combatants (EOKA) and their aim is unification or enosis with Greece. Their leaders included Cypriot Archbishop Makarios.

POLIO VACCINES
U.S. physician and microbiologist Jonas Salk (1914–1995) announces the development of a vaccine against poliomyelitis, which is rife in the United States. It is an injectable vaccine and is given a large clinical trial. U.S. virologist Albert Sabin (1906–1993) has also developed a vaccine against poliomyelitis. It is an oral vaccine, which can be taken on a sugar lump.

HOWL: ANTHEM OF THE BEAT GENERATION
American beat poet Allen Ginsberg (1926–1997) has published *Howl*. A long poem, it is a rejection of material values and an elegy for the American dream. With its publication, a group of young writers known as the Beat Generation now become widely known.

MODERN STYLE CHAPEL
French architect Le Corbusier completes his chapel of Notre Dame du Haut in Ronchamp, France. With its curved walls clad in white concrete and its great billowing roof, it brings a new, plastic language to modern architecture.

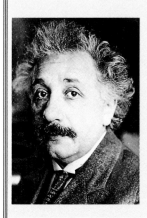

LEFT: The newly developed vaccine against poliomyelitis is expected to prevent death and disablement from the disease that causes infantile paralysis, as seen above.

JAMES BYRON DEAN
(1931–1955)

The young American actor James Dean has been killed in a car crash. He made his name with the film *East of Eden* (1955), which was swiftly followed by *Rebel Without a Cause*. He began his acting career while studying at California University and he trained at the Actor's Studio. His last film, *Giant*, will be released next year.

ALBERT EINSTEIN
(1879–1955)

Almost certainly the greatest scientist of our age, Albert Einstein has died. His work on the theory of relativity, published in 1905 and 1916, explained problems that had been waiting to be solved since Newton. It gained him the Nobel Prize in 1921. German-born, he eventually became a citizen of the United States.

CHARLES "BIRD" PARKER
(1920–1955)

The great Kansas-born tenor and alto sax player, Charlie Parker, has died from complications as a result of his lifelong addiction to heroin and alcohol. A much admired improviser, he was one of the pioneers of the bebop style and had a strong influence on the development of jazz in the 1940s. He played in quintets with musicians such as trumpeters Dizzy Gillespie and Miles Davis, and pianists Al Haig and Duke Jordan.

ABOVE: Television becomes the focal point of home entertainment for most Western families.

ABOVE: The great jazz clarinet player, Benny Goodman.

BELOW: The USS *Nautilus* is the American Navy's first submarine to be driven by nuclear power.

HOVERCRAFT PATENTED
English radio engineer and boat designer Christopher Cockerell (1910–1999) patents the hovercraft, also known as an air cushion vehicle or ACV.

PERON IS BANISHED
Rebel forces seize control of the Argentine military in September, forcing President Juan Peron into hiding. Rather than bring attention to him through a public trial, the new junta grants Peron asylum and sends him to Paraguay.

U.S.S.R. TESTS HYDROGEN BOMB
The Soviet Union follows America's testing of a hydrogen bomb with one of their own, in November. The bomb is equal to one million tons of TNT, or one megaton.

MARY MCLEOD BETHUNE
(1875–1955)

The distinguished educator, Mary Mcleod Bethune, has died at the age of 79. She established the Daytona Institute, the first boarding school for black girls, which later became Bethune-Cookman College. She went on to form the National Council of Negro Women in 1935. She advised President Franklin Delano Roosevelt on numerous issues and eventually became a member of his Black Cabinet. In 1940, she became vice president of the NAACP.

ABOVE: The ultramodern St. Louis Airport Terminal designed by the Missouri-based architects Hellmuth, Yamasaki, and Leinweber.

MAU MAU REBELLION ENDS

In Kenya, an amnesty by the British government calms the Mau Mau rebellion against British rule. The Mau Mau, a secret society of the Kikuyu tribe, was formed in 1948 and in 1952 began a campaign of arson and killings to drive whites off Kikuyu land and force the British to leave Kenya. Their leader, Jomo Kenyatta (1889–1978), was imprisoned. The Mau Mau began to decline after a massacre at Lari in the Rift Valley, in March 1953, killed more than 80 people, mostly African. In total, more than 11,000 Mau Mau members have been killed in the uprising, mainly by fellow Africans.

AUSTRIAN INDEPENDENCE RESTORED

The four occupying powers, United States, Soviet Union, Britain, and France, agree to restore Austrian independence within its 1937 frontiers. In return for its neutrality, a ban is put on any *Anschluss* or unity with Germany, and a ban on any return of the Hapsburg monarchy. The treaty removes one of the major irritants in relations between East and West in Europe.

ANTIPROTONS

Scientists detect antiprotons, short-lived subatomic particles that are identical to protons, but with negative electrical charges.

FIFTIES FASHION

The Fifties see an explosion of new fashion ideas, celebrating Western women's growing independence and freedom of choice, as well as reflecting increasing affluence.

LEFT: Casual elegance is the keynote of Fifties fashion.

ABOVE: Postwar women are entering the workforce and smart clothes for the office are in demand.

ABOVE AND RIGHT: After the war decade, fashion reflects the desire for luxury without sacrificing women's newfound independence.

ABOVE: More people can now afford easy wear for their vacations.

CRISIS IN SUEZ AND REVOLT IN HUNGARY

Soviet tanks put down a prodemocracy uprising in Hungary, despite appeals by Hungary to the United Nations. World political tensions rise during the Suez Crisis and Israel attacks Egypt. Fidel Castro and his followers begin guerrilla warfare against the Batista regime in Cuba. In the fields of medicine and science, kidney dialysis begins and astronomers measure the surface temperature of the planet Venus. Popular music includes hits from *My Fair Lady* and Elvis Presley's "Heartbreak Hotel."

1956

Jan	1	Sudan is declared an independent republic
	26	Winter Games are televised in Italy
Feb	29	Soviet premier Nikita Khrushchev denounces Stalin's policies
Mar	2	Morocco becomes independent from France
	9	Archbishop Makarios deported from Cyprus
	20	Tunisia becomes independent from France
Apr	25	Heavyweight champion Rocky Marciano retires undefeated
June	29	Playwright Arthur Miller and actress Marilyn Monroe are wed
July	26	President Nasser of Egypt nationalizes the Suez Canal
Aug	14	German playwright and director Bertolt Brecht dies
Oct	23	Demonstrations in Hungary call for democratic government
	24	Imre Nagy is appointed Hungarian prime minister
	29	Israeli forces invade Sinai Peninsula
Nov	1	Emergency session of the United Nations to discuss Suez Crisis
	2	Hungarian government appeals to U.N. for assistance against Soviet invasion
	5	British paratroopers land in Port Said, Egypt in defiance of a U.N. resolution
	20	Castro and followers land in Cuba to begin guerrilla war against Batista
Dec	5	British and French forces begin to withdraw from Egypt

FORMER COLONIES INDEPENDENT

The former Anglo-Egyptian colony of Sudan becomes independent from Britain in January. Morocco and Tunisia receive their independence from France in March.

SUEZ CRISIS

In July, Egyptian President Nasser (1918–1970) nationalizes the Anglo-French Suez Canal Company, which controls the vital waterway between the Mediterranean and Red Sea. The move is strongly opposed by Britain. Nasser makes the move after Britain and the United States refused to provide funds to build the Aswan Dam across the Nile, which is designed to increase Egypt's cultivable land by more than half and to provide hydroelectricity. The dam is later built with Soviet aid. In November, in collusion with the Israelis, the British and French launch an airborne and amphibious attack to seize the Suez Canal. Operationally, the landings are a complete success, but politically they are a disaster. The U.N. votes for a cease-fire after international condemnation of the Anglo-French invasion, led by the United States. Britain and France are obliged to halt their attacks and withdraw in December. As a result of the debacle, the British prime minister, Anthony Eden, resigns.

RIGHT: Anti-government demonstrators in Salonika, Greece, use rolls of newsprint as roadblocks against the Army's armored cars.

STALIN DENOUNCED

Nikita Khrushchev, now in firm control of the Soviet Union, denounces Stalin at a closed session of the Communist Party Congress. The break with Stalinism leads to a relaxation of state control and terror in the Soviet Union and some Eastern European nations begin to loosen their ties with the Soviet Union.

MAKARIOS DEPORTED

Britain deports Archbishop Makarios and other Greek Cypriot leaders to the Seychelles on suspicion of involvement with EOKA terrorists fighting to unite Cyprus, a British colony, with Greece. Conflict between Greeks and Turks on the island has been growing for some years as the Greeks seek union with Greece and the Turks seek to protect their rights.

ARAB-ISRAELI WAR

In October, in a prearranged secret move with the British and French governments, the small but well-equipped and well-trained Israeli army attacks Egyptian forces in the Sinai who have been threatening Israel's access to the Red Sea from Eilat. In a lightning campaign, they capture the Sinai Peninsula plus huge quantities of Egyptian military equipment and large numbers of prisoners. The Franco-British intervention at Suez was ostensibly a peacekeeping operation to separate the Israeli and Egyptian forces.

HEARTBREAK HOTEL

Rock star Elvis Presley records bestselling "Heartbreak Hotel" and makes his film debut in *Love Me Tender*. In the United States, he appears live on T.V. on the Ed Sullivan Show. His fans adore him but some criticize his "provocative" movements.

ABOVE: Demonstrators fill the streets of Polish cities, reflecting growing unrest that culminates in the Poznan riots.

ABOVE: Preparations for the American expedition to the South Pole, as the advance survey party leaves the supply ship anchored at McMurdo Sound.

LONG DAY'S JOURNEY
U.S. playwright Eugene O'Neill's play, *Long Day's Journey into Night*, is performed. A family tragedy, partly based on the writer's own life, it depicts the disintegration of the relationships between the ex-actor James Tyrone, his drug addicted wife Mary, and their two sons.

MY FAIR LADY
Alan Jay Lerner and Frederick Loewe's musical, *My Fair Lady*, opens on Broadway. Based on George Bernard Shaw's play *Pygmalion*, it is a smash success.

KITCHEN SINK DRAMA
The play *Look Back in Anger*, by British writer John Osborne (1929–1994), is performed. It centers on an "angry young man," Jimmy Porter, who becomes the archetype of a generation. The play is typical of so-called British "kitchen sink dramas" which feature working class or lower middle class domestic settings.

INTERFERON
British virologist Alick Isaacs and a Swiss colleague, Jean Lindenmann, discover interferon, a protective substance produced in cells when they are infected by viruses.

MELBOURNE GAMES
This year's Olympic Games are in Melbourne, Australia, the first to be held in the southern hemisphere. They are affected by a series of political boycotts, in the wake of the Suez crisis and the Soviet invasion of Hungary. Soviet gymnast Larissa Latynina wins four golds, a silver, and a bronze. The hosts sweep the board in the swimming events. The Soviet Union won the most medals surpassing the United States by a total of 30.

CUBAN REBELS
Having reassembled, Fidel Castro and his followers, who include Castro's brother Raul and Che Guevara (1928–1967), land in Cuba, from the yacht *Gramma*. They begin a campaign of guerrilla war to overthrow the dictatorial government of President Batista. As volunteers join Castro's group in the Sierra Maestra, he is able to go on the offensive.

VIDEOTAPE BEGINS
The Ampex Company of California builds the first commercial videotape machine. The machine will use 2.5 inch tape.

ABOVE: The Melbourne Olympic Games attract huge crowds from all over the world.

THE SEVENTH SEAL

Starring actor Max von Sydow, *The Seventh Seal* is the latest film by Swedish film director Ingmar Bergman (b. 1918). Including a game of chess between Death and a knight, who argues the goodness of humanity, the film establishes Bergman's reputation as a major force in the cinema.

NEUTRINOS DETECTED

U.S. physicists Frederick Reines and Clyde Lorrain detect the subatomic particles neutrinos and antineutrinos.

TRANSATLANTIC PHONE CABLE

The first cable, called TAT 1, to carry telephone calls is laid across the Atlantic between Scotland and Newfoundland. It contains 51 repeaters along its 2,263 mile length to boost the signal.

TELEVISED GAMES

The first televised Winter Games sees action broadcast from Cortina d'Ampezzo in Italy. The Seventh Olympiad is rescued by heavy snow on the opening day. On the rink, the Soviets end Canadian domination of ice hockey.

KIDNEY DIALYSIS BEGINS

The kidney dialysis machine, which was invented by Dutch physician Willem J. Kolff (b. 1911) in 1943, comes into general use in America. The machine uses a membrane to filter out impurities from the blood.

VENUS IS HOT STUFF

American astronomers studying the microwaves emitted from the planet Venus discover its surface temperature is far above the boiling point of water. In 1962, a space probe measures it at 900°F.

CELL MESSENGERS FOUND

Scientists studying cells discover messenger RNA (ribonucleic acid). This makes a reverse copy of the plans for making a protein from the DNA of that protein and serves as a mold for making a new one.

BREASTFEEDING ENCOURAGED

The La Lèche League is founded at Franklin Park, Illinois, to encourage breastfeeding. Breast milk has been found to give babies additional protection against disease.

NO MORE MISTAKES

Bette Nesmith, an American housewife, converts her cottage industry selling Mistake Out (a white paint preparation to blank out typing errors) to local typists, into a national corporation named Liquid Paper, Inc.

ABSTRACT ARTIST DIES

Abstract Expressionist painter Jackson Pollock was killed in a single-car crash. His original technique, called the "drip" paintings, is recognized as a benchmark in modern art. The public, however, found it cryptic and referred to him as "Jack the Dripper."

ANDREA DORIA SINKS

The Swedish ocean liner *Stockholm* collided with the Italian ship *Andrea Doria* during heavy fog south of Nantucket, killing 51 people. The *Andrea Doria* sunk within 11 hours, while the *Stockholm* was able to make it back to port.

Melbourne Olympic highlights include the U.K.'s Chris Brasher winning the 3,000m steeplechase (top) and American Milt Campbell (above) taking the decathlon gold.

ABOVE: A huge statue of Stalin is pulled down and dragged through the streets of Budapest during the anti-Soviet riots.

ABOVE: The Hungarian flag is draped over the body of a freedom fighter.

RIGHT: A Hungarian resistance fighter explains how to use a Molotov cocktail.

THE HUNGARIAN UPRISING

Demonstrations break out in Budapest against Soviet domination. Hungary has been part of the Communist bloc since 1946. The former Hungarian prime minister, Imre Nagy, who was forced out of office in February 1955, returns to power promising reform after demonstrators call for democratic government and the withdrawal of Soviet troops. However, demonstrations lead to a wider uprising against the Soviet Union. Nagy forms a government including non-Communists and takes Hungary out of the Warsaw Pact, appealing for Western aid against any Soviet invasion. However, in November, Moscow sends 2,500 tanks and armored vehicles and 200,000 troops into Hungary. Street fighting erupts in Budapest, but the Hungarians are crushed and 12,000 people are killed. Nagy is deposed in favor of János Kádár, who changes sides to head the new government. Nagy is executed after a secret trial in June 1958.

ABOVE: Students pose in front of Budapest University with their machine guns during the October Revolution, having taken up arms against the threat of Soviet domination.

RIGHT: In Mexico, workers demonstrate in support of the Hungarian revolutionaries.

SPUTNIKS ORBIT THE EARTH

The Space Race gets under way as the Russians launch the world's first artificial satellites: *Sputnik I* and *Sputnik II*. *Sputnik II* carries a little dog, Laika, and captures the imagination of the world. Free trade comes closer in Europe as various countries form the European Common Market. U.S. troops are sent to Little Rock, Arkansas, to enforce racial integration in the schools. *West Side Story* opens on Broadway.

1957

Jan 10 Queen Elizabeth II names Conservative Party member Harold Macmillan as the new Prime Minister

14 Actor Humphrey Bogart dies of cancer at the age of 57

22 Israeli forces make a complete withdrawal from the Sinai Peninsula, but remain in the Gaza Strip

Feb 6 Gold Coast becomes independent as Ghana

Mar 25 Treaty of Rome sets up European Common Market

28 Britain releases Archbishop Makarios

May 2 Anti-communist Senator Joseph McCarthy dies at the age of 48

July 6 Althea Gibson, U.S. tennis player, becomes first black player to win Wimbledon singles

Aug 31 Malaya gains independence from Britain

Sep 25 Schools desegregate in Little Rock, Arkansas, after U.S. troops arrive

26 The musical *West Side Story* opens on Broadway

Oct 4 Russians launch the world's first man-made satellite, Sputnik I

24 French fashion designer Christian Dior dies at the age of 52

Nov 3 Russians launch Sputnik II which carries a dog named Laika

25 Mexican mural painter Diego Rivera dies at the age of 72

Dec 18 The nation's first atomic power plant opens in Shippingport, Pennsylvania

28 The Baltimore Colts defeat the New York Giants to win the NFL title

ABOVE: Althea Gibson receives a rapturous welcome on her return from winning the Women's Tennis Championship at Wimbledon.

EUROPEAN COMMON MARKET

France, West Germany, Netherlands, Belgium, Luxembourg, and Italy sign the Treaty of Rome, setting up the European Common Market, later the European Economic Union (EEC). Its aim is the free movement of goods, money, and people through its member nations. The Treaty also sets up the European Atomic Energy Authority (Euratom).

FIRST SPUTNIKS

Sputnik I, the world's first man-made Earth satellite, is successfully launched by the Soviet Union on the 50th anniversary of the Russian Revolution. A month later they launch Sputnik II, which carries the first animal into space, a female dog called Laika. This is in preparation for sending humans into space.

LITTLE ROCK

U.S. federal paratroopers are sent in to enforce integration of local schools in Little Rock, Arkansas, after black pupils are refused admission to the Central High School. Arkansas governor Orval Faubus uses the state militia to bar their entry. The action causes outrage in the southern states against the federal government.

MALAYA INDEPENDENT

The Federation of Malaya gains its independence from Britain, the last major British Asian colony to do so.

GOLD COAST INDEPENDENT

The British colony of the Gold Coast becomes the first black African state to win its independence from European rule as Ghana, under the charismatic leadership of Kwame Nkrumah (1909–1972).

DOCTOR ZHIVAGO

Russian author Boris Pasternak (1890–1960) publishes his novel, *Doctor Zhivago*, in Italy because it will not be published in his native U.S.S.R. An account of Russia and its intelligentsia during the revolutionary period, the novel is a rapid success. The following year, Pasternak is awarded the Nobel Prize for Literature.

ON THE ROAD

American author Jack Kerouac (1922–1969) publishes his partly autobiographical novel *On the Road*. Fast-moving and loosely structured, the style of the novel reflects the travels and life of the central character, writer Sal Paradise. It puts Kerouac on the literary map and makes him, together with writers Alan Ginsberg and William Burroughs, a leading figure of the Beat Generation. Followers of Beat Generation philosophy reject social and artistic conventions, favor progressive jazz, and explore mystical experiences offered by Eastern religions.

PALAZETTO DEL SPORT

Italian architect Pier Luigi Nervi (1891–1979) designs the Palazetto del Sport for the 1960 Olympic Games to be held in Rome. The stadium is made of prefabricated parts, including striking concrete Y-frames. It enables the construction of the main dome, 200 feet in diameter, to be completed in only 40 days.

WEST SIDE STORY

American conductor and composer Leonard Bernstein's musical *West Side Story* has opened on Broadway. An adaptation of *Romeo and Juliet*, the exciting musical is set among the street gangs of New York City. U.S. composer Stephen Sondheim has written the lyrics, including popular favorites "America" and "Maria."

VOSS

The Australian novelist Patrick White (1912–1990) publishes *Voss*, a novel about a German explorer's bid to lead an expedition across Australia. It brings him international recognition.

VELCRO PATENTED

Swiss inventor Georges de Mestral patents Velcro™, the cling fabric fastener based on the cocklebur principle. It has taken him 17 years to perfect.

RADIO TELESCOPE

A radio telescope, with a steerable dish 249 feet across, comes into operation at Jodrell Bank, Cheshire, England. It will be used by astronomers at the University of Manchester.

ABOVE: Screen icons Elizabeth Taylor and James Dean in *Giant*, a story of lust and oil in Texas, released the year after Dean's death.

ABOVE: In the People's Republic of China, the Cultural Revolution means that everyone does hard physical work.

PACEMAKER

U.S. physician Clarence Lillehei devises a pacemaker small enough to be inserted in a patient's body and control a heart that is beating irregularly.

NUCLEAR ACCIDENTS

Two nuclear accidents release radioactivity into the atmosphere. One occurs at Windscale nuclear power plant in the U.K. and the other in a Russian nuclear waste storage facility in the Ural Mountains.

PSYCHOLINGUISTICS

The psychology of language, or psycholinguistics, is galvanized by the publication of *Syntactic Structures* by Noam Chomsky (b. 1928). He theorizes that language began, and starts in children, not with sounds but with rudimentary sentences whose structure follows rules common to all languages.

GRAND PRIX WINNER

At the age of 46, Juan Manuel Fangio (1911–1995) wins a record fifth Grand Prix World Championship with a stunning victory in the German Grand Prix. The Argentinian, driving a Maserati, smashes the lap record ten times during the race.

FATS CAUSE HEART DISEASE

A paper by University of Minnesota nutritionist Ancel Keys, published in the *Journal of the American Medical Association*, establishes a connection between diets high in animal fats and heart disease.

WOLFENDEN REPORT

In the United Kingdom, the Report of the Home Office Committee on Homosexual Offenses and Prostitution by Sir John Wolfenden, chancellor of Reading University, unexpectedly recommends an end to punitive laws against homosexual acts between consenting adults.

DODGERS TO MOVE

Walter O'Malley, president of the Brooklyn Dodgers, announces the team is moving from New York City to Los Angeles. The news outrages Dodgers fans, but is the first of many such transfers as baseball expansion begins.

CHRISTIAN DIOR
(1905–1957)

Christian Dior, the French couturier who launched the postwar "New Look" in Paris in 1947, has died. The House of Dior also introduced the A-line, the sack dress, and created several well-known perfumes, including "Miss Dior."

JOSEPH RAYMOND MCCARTHY
(1909–1957)

The fanatical anti-Communist American Republican, Senator Joseph (Joe) McCarthy, has died. Since 1950, he had been conducting a witch-hunt among citizens and officials, becoming chairman of the so-called House Committee on Un-American Activities in 1953. Many prominent intellectuals and actors have been among those accused of being Communists. In 1954, McCarthy was censured by the Senate for his methods, but he remained rabidly anti-Communist to the end.

DIEGO RIVERA
(1886–1957)

Mexican painter Diego Rivera has died. His powerful works, which consist largely of mural paintings in public buildings in both Mexico and the United States, were inspired by folk art and his revolutionary beliefs. His paintings have sometimes caused a stir because of their ideological content.

ABOVE: U.S. President Eisenhower, reelected in 1956, is pictured here talking to Lyndon Johnson.

ABOVE: Future astronaut John H. Glenn celebrates a nonstop flight around the world in a B-52 bomber.

ABOVE: Archaeologists in Iraq unearth one of the biggest finds of inscribed Sumerian clay tablets ever discovered.

MARCHING AGAINST THE BOMB

The United States launches *Explorer I* into space, the first of a series of science satellites. Anti-nuclear feeling finds a voice as the Campaign for Nuclear Disarmament is formed. In the face of continuing Algerian problems, Charles de Gaulle becomes president of France. The new contraceptive pill goes on sale in the United States with the potential for transforming women's lives. Elvis is inducted into the Army, and Barbie is born.

1958

Jan	**3**	A New Zealand expedition led by Mt. Everest Climber Edmund Hillary, reaches the South Pole
Feb	**1**	United States launches its first space satellite, the *Explorer I*. It will orbit the earth every 114 minutes
	17	CND formed in London with the slogan "Ban the Bomb"
Mar	**24**	Elvis Presley begins two years of military service
	27	Nikita Khrushchev becomes Premier of the Soviet Union
Apr	**7**	CND holds first "Aldermaston March" from London to Aldermaston nuclear research station
May	**19**	New York Democratic Congressman Adam Clayton Powell is charged with income tax evasion
May	**31**	Algerian crisis forces recall of Charles de Gaulle
June	**16**	Former Hungarian Premier Imre Nagy is executed
July	**14**	King Hussein of Jordan assumes power as head of Arab Federation
	15	President Eisenhower sends troops to Lebanon
	31	A coup d'etat in Iraq organized by military leaders, kills King Faisal, the Premier, and the Crown Prince
Sep	**9**	Race riots flare in the Notting Hill district in London
Oct	**2**	Guinea declared an independent republic
Dec	**21**	Charles de Gaulle is elected president of France

DE GAULLE COMES TO POWER

Trouble continues in Algeria. After a revolt by French settlers in Algeria against moves by the French government to negotiate with the Algerian Nationalist forces, the French government falls and Charles de Gaulle (1890–1970) takes power. He takes emergency powers for six months and draws up a new constitution, which ends the unstable Fourth Republic and establishes the Fifth Republic with strong presidential powers. In December, de Gaulle becomes president of France, and promises talks with the Algerian rebels.

CND FORMED

Anti-nuclear protesters form the Campaign for Nuclear Disarmament (CND) at a rally in London, addressed by the philosopher Bertrand Russell (1872–1970). They march from London to the nuclear research establishment at Aldermaston to protest against Britain's nuclear capacity. Other CND anti-nuclear organizations are formed around the world.

KING FAISAL OVERTHROWN

In Iraq, the army overthrows the pro-Western monarchy of King Faisal, destabilizing the region. In response, U.S. troops land in Lebanon and British troops land in Jordan to support these governments against possible coup attempts.

SEAGRAM BUILDING

A new office building, the Seagram Building in New York City, is the ultimate modern tower. It is restrained in its details and based on a glass and metal structure. Designed by Mies van der Rohe (1886–1969) and Philip Johnson (b. 1906), the building's detail and high-quality material make it extremely distinctive.

SUB UNDER ARCTIC OCEAN

U.S. nuclear submarine *Nautilus*, launched in 1955, sails under the Arctic Ocean ice cap. It is the first underwater voyage from the Pacific to the Atlantic beneath the North Polar ice cap.

ABOVE: Teenagers, with their own music, style, crazes, and language, are the phenomenon of the 1950s in America and all over Europe.

GUINEA INDEPENDENT

Prime Minister Sekou Toure (1922–1984) declares Guinea an independent republic in the French West African colony and leaves the new French community. Other French colonies remain tied to France.

THE FIRE RAISERS

A play, *The Fire Raisers*, by architect and writer Max Frisch, is performed. It targets the complacency of the middle classes in the person of a man who will tolerate even the burning down of his own home.

BRILLIANT BRAZIL

The World Cup takes place in Sweden and marks the arrival of Brazilian player Pelé, the greatest player of the world's most popular game. He scores six goals in the tournament and Brazil takes home the title, beating the hosts 5–2 in the final.

BARBIE IS BORN

The Barbie doll is created in the United States by Mattel. A revised version of an earlier doll, she is given a teenage fashion model look and a complete, up-to-date wardrobe is designed for her 1959 launch.

NEW ZEALAND ARRIVES FIRST

Edmund Hillary's New Zealand team beats Vivian Fuchs's British team overland to the South Pole. Hillary's party sets out from McMurdo Sound and the British from the Vansee Sea. As a contribution to the International Geophysical Year, Britain's team goes on to make the first transantarctic crossing.

AMERICAN EXPRESS

The Bank of America launches American Express, the first-ever credit card. By December, it is being used by some 500,000 people.

THE LEOPARD

The only novel by Sicilian prince Giuseppe di Lampedusa (1896–1957) is published posthumously. Entitled *The Leopard*, it describes how a noble family in Sicily responds to changes after Italy annexes the island in 1860.

ABOVE: Marian Anderson, American contralto, in a scene from *The Lady from Philadelphia.*

ABOVE: Composer and conductor Leonard Bernstein conducting a rehearsal of the New York Philharmonic Symphony Orchestra.

NOBELIUM PRODUCED

Element 102, nobelium, is artificially created by American scientists. It is the ninth and last element with which Glenn T. Seaborg is involved.

VAN ALLEN BELTS

At the suggestion of physicist James Van Allen (b. 1914), U.S. satellite Explorer 4 carries radiation counters heavily shielded with lead. They register cosmic rays, showing that there are belts of very high radiation, later called the Van Allen Belts.

EXPLORER I

The United States follows the Soviet Union and sends its first artificial satellite, *Explorer I*, into space. The launch rocket has been developed by Werner von Braun, previously head of Germany's V-2 program. *Explorer I* is the first in a series of U.S. scientific satellites.

NIXON ABUSED ON LATIN AMERICA TOUR

Vice President Nixon cut short his goodwill tour to Latin America after being hit with stones and spat upon in Lima, Peru and requiring military protection amid violence in Caracas, Venezuela. The trouble in both countries was instigated by factions of the Communist Party.

MAJOR LEAGUE MOVES FROM NYC

The Brooklyn Dodgers have officially departed Ebbets Field to begin playing in Los Angeles this season and the New York Giants have deserted the Polo Grounds for their new home in San Francisco.

FORMER HUNGARIAN PREMIER EXECUTED

Premier Imre Nagy was kidnapped in 1956 by pro-Soviet forces, tried and found guilty behind closed doors in Romania, and returned this year to be hanged.

SEXUAL EQUALITY

The Netherlands COC (Cultuur-en-Ontspannings Centrum) sponsors the fifth International Conference on Sexual Equality. The Conference offers a beacon of rational support for lesbian and gay organizations elsewhere in Europe. where they are suppressed and persecuted.

BIRTH PILL

The Pill, the first oral contraceptive for women. is marketed in the United States. Containing artificial hormones estrogen and progesterone, it prevents conception by simulating pregnancy. The pill has been developed by Gregory Pincus who was visited by the feminist Margaret Sanger in 1951. Pincus produced the Pill in association with Hudson Hoagland and Min-Cheh Chang in 1954.

HULA HOOP AND SKATEBOARD CRAZE

New crazes sweep the United States when the hula hoop, launched by Arthur Melin and Richard Knerr. and the skateboard, invented by Bill and Mark Richards, appear in California.

STEREO RECORDING

Record companies in the United States and Britain issue the first stereophonic records.

UNDERSTANDING SOCIAL BEHAVIOR

Claude Levi-Strauss, Belgian-born anthropologist and professor of ethnology at the University of Paris. publishes *Structural Anthropology*. He theorizes that societies have a similar structure that reflects the way myths are created. and these, when accurately understood, will enable us to understand their behavior.

POLYGAMY RESTRICTED

The government of newly independent Morocco liberalizes the law in favor of women, granting women the right to choose their own husbands and restricting polygamy.

XEROX GOES COMMERCIAL

The first commercial Xerox copier goes on sale. Invented in 1947, it makes dry copies of documents.

LYCRA LAUNCHED

In the United States, Du Pont launches Lycra. the first of the Spandex fibers or man-made elastics.

NASA VICTORY

NASA officials have reported the first successful launching of an Intercontinental Ballistic Missile. This comes one month after the failure of a Pioneer satellite that burned up during its attempt to orbit the moon.

PASTERNAK DECLINES NOBEL PRIZE

Succumbing to Soviet pressure. Russian Boris Pasternak refuses the Nobel Prize for his novel "Dr. Zhivago."

ABOVE: Robots seize the imagination. American Sherwood Fuehrer, age fourteen, invents a life-sized robot called Gizmo, which he can maneuver with a remote control.

ABOVE: Jerry Lee Lewis, a charismatic singer and pianist who outrages the Establishment.

CASTRO TAKES CONTROL IN CUBA

In Cuba, Fidel Castro succeeds in toppling Batista to take over the Cuban government. The Dalai Lama, Tibet's spiritual leader, flees Chinese-occupied Tibet. The oldest known hominid remains are found in Africa. The new Guggenheim Museum in New York City is opened, but its brilliant architect, Frank Lloyd Wright, dies just before completion. Soviet spacecraft crash-land on the Moon and send back the first photographs of its dark side.

1959

Jan	1	Batista resigns and then flees Cuba, following guerrilla campaign
	16	Castro enters Havana and sets up provisional government
Mar	20	Tibetan uprising against Chinese. Dalai Lama is smuggled out of Tibet
Apr	3	Dalai Lama reaches India from Chinese-occupied Tibet
	9	Frank Lloyd Wright dies at age 92
June	26	St. Lawrence Seaway opens
July	17	The Leakey's, British anthropologists, discover *Homo habilis* in Olduvai Gorge, Tanzania
Aug	7	Chinese forces enter northeast India
Oct	26	Soviet spacecraft films dark side of the Moon

Nov	10	United Nations condemns apartheid in South Africa
	20	The "Seven" set up European Free Trade Agreement (EFTA)
Dec	1	Antarctic Treaty signed by 12 nations keeps Antarctic free of territorial or military claims

ABOVE: Emperor penguins and the USS *Glacier* in Antarctica.

ABOVE: A new type of radio telescope built by Australian astronomer Dr. Ronald Bracewell. BELOW: The bows of the cruiser USS *Long Beach*, the U.S. Navy's first nuclear-powered surface ship, stand tall in the naval shipyard at Quincy, Massachusetts.

CASTRO IN POWER

Fidel Castro takes power in Cuba after Batista flees into exile to the Dominican Republic. The takeover comes at the end of an insurrection that has lasted for more than two years. Dr. Manuel Urratia is proclaimed provisional president of Cuba with Castro as prime minister.

DALAI LAMA FLEES

A rising against Chinese rule is repressed by the Chinese army and the Dalai Lama. Tibet's Buddhist spiritual leader is smuggled out of Tibet and flees into exile in India, where he appeals for U.N. intervention to secure the independence of Tibet.

RWANDAN CIVIL WAR

Civil war breaks out in Rwanda, which has recently been granted self-government by Belgium, the colonial power. The ruling Tutsi people, who make up only a small percentage of the population, have been attacked by the Hutu, who make up 85 per cent of the population. A Hutu-dominated republic is proclaimed following a U.N. supervised vote. When armed Tutsi *emigrés* attack the new nation, they are driven off and many Tutsi are massacred in reprisal.

DISPUTE OVER INDIA/CHINA BORDER

A border dispute breaks out in the Himalayas between India and China, prompted by China's belief that the British-designated border is no longer valid.

BUDDY (CHARLES HARDIN) HOLLY (1936–1959)

Charles Hardin, the singer better known as Buddy Holly, has died in a plane crash while in route to his next show in Fargo, North Dakota. The fans of the American rock and roller will be devastated. He and his band, the Crickets, established the new standard lineup of two guitars, bass, and drums. Also killed in the crash were singers Richie Valens and J.P. "Big Bopper" Richardson.

FRANK LLOYD WRIGHT (1867–1959)

The outstanding American modern architect, Frank Lloyd Wright, has died in his 90s. He had been designing innovative buildings during the entire century. His greatest works include the prairie-style Robie House (1908), the international modernist style Fallingwater (1937), and office structures such as the Johnson Wax Office Building (1936). He had almost completed the Guggenheim Museum in New York City at the time of his death.

NOUVELLE VAGUE

French film director Alain Resnais (b. 1922) premieres his first full-length film, *Hiroshima Mon Amour*. Set in Hiroshima, it establishes Resnais as a leading member of the *Nouvelle Vague* (New Wave). This year too, French film director Jean Luc Godard (b. 1930) releases his first full-length film, *A Bout de Souffle*. The film is shot without a script, indicating Godard's emphasis on improvisatory techniques.

SYNTHESIZER

The Radio Corporation of America invents the synthesizer, an electronic instrument which can imitate the sounds of many traditional instruments and also make new technical sounds.

STOCK CAR RACING

The most prestigious race in American stock car racing is born at Daytona International Speedway in Florida. Lee Petty wins the first Daytona 500 in an Oldsmobile.

ST. LAWRENCE SEAWAY

The St. Lawrence Seaway, a system of rivers, lakes, and canals that enables oceangoing ships to carry cargoes to and from the Great Lakes of North America, opens.

SOME LIKE IT HOT

U.S. film actress Marilyn Monroe (1926–1962) stars as singer Sugar Kane in a new Billy Wilder film, *Some Like it Hot*. The film, which is a lively comedy, confirms her status as an international star.

ABOVE: Dog models in Soviet rocket chambers designed to carry real canines on short space flights. Two dogs do in fact make the trip and return safely to earth.

GUGGENHEIM MUSEUM

With its unique spiral design, the new Guggenheim Museum in New York City is one of the most striking modern buildings. The paintings are hung beside a continuous spiral ramp. Visitors will take the elevator to the top, walk down, and hopefully minimize "museum fatigue" in the process.

RHINOCEROS

Romanian-born dramatist Eugene Ionesco (1912–94) creates "anti-plays," in which a world of nightmare fuses with farce. His latest is *Rhinoceros*, in which the cast turn one by one into rhinoceroses, interpreted by most critics as the image of a totalitarian takeover.

SWISS WOMEN REJECTED

The Swiss electorate votes to reject a proposed amendment to the constitution to permit women to vote in national elections and run for national office.

THE TIN DRUM

German novelist Günter Grass (b. 1927) publishes *The Tin Drum*. The novel, which features the hunchback Oskar who decides to stop growing in infancy, becomes a bestseller in Germany. Its narrative seems to sum up the history of Germany during the twentieth century.

HANDY MAN FOUND

British anthropologists Louis and Mary Leakey discover, in Olduvai Gorge, Tanzania, fossils of the earliest human species. The species is named *Homo habilis*, "Handy Man," and lived two million years ago. Stone tools found on the site are the earliest implements discovered to date.

BULGING EARTH

The U.S. satellite *Vanguard 1* makes thousands of orbits of the Earth and shows that the planet is about 25 feet fatter in the south than in the north.

FIRST TRIP TO THE MOON

Lunar II, an unmanned Soviet spacecraft, becomes the first space probe to crash-land on the Moon. On the journey, it confirms the existence of the solar wind, a flow of gases from the Sun. Later this year, *Lunar III* orbits the Moon and transmits pictures of its dark side, the side never before seen from Earth.

ABOVE: An East German bread vendor stands beside a poster of Soviet premier Nikita Khrushchev shaking hands with East Germany's Communist leader Walter Ulbricht.

ANTARCTICA

The Antarctic Treaty is signed by 12 nations, including the U.S., Britain and the U.S.S.R. It suspends all territorial and military claims, restricts exploration of the Antarctic to peaceful purposes only, and establishes the continent south of 60° as a preserve for scientific research. The treaty lasts until 1989, then it is renewed.

EFTA

Seven European countries, including Sweden, Norway, Denmark, Britain, Portugal, Austria, and Switzerland, set up the European Free Trade Area (EFTA) to rival the EEC.

JOHN FOSTER DULLES
(1888–1959)

American Republican politician John Foster Dulles has died of cancer. As Secretary of State in the 1950s, he devoted his energies to alerting the world to the threat of Communism, and at the same time contributing to the rise of Cold War tension.

BILLIE (ELEANOR FAGANA) HOLIDAY
(1915–1959)

American jazz singer Billie Holiday, also known as Lady Day, has died. She sang with leading jazz artists such as Benny Goodman, Lester Young, Count Basie, and Louis Armstrong. She leaves the world recordings of songs such as "Easy Living" (1937), which are bound to endure.

ABOVE: India's Prime Minister Jawaharlal Nehru at the inauguration of the Hirakud Dam, one of several projects designed to boost food production through irrigation and to provide hydroelectric power for India's developing industry.

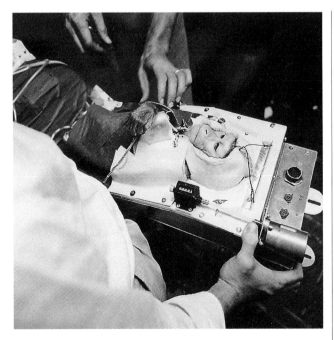

ABOVE: Astronaut monkeys provide important information about the biomedical factors affecting manned space flight.

ABOVE: Self-propelled anti-aircraft guns pass the reviewing stand at the May Day parade in East Berlin.

WINNERS AND ACHIEVERS OF THE 1950s

ACADEMY AWARDS
The Academy of Motion Picture Arts and Sciences was founded in 1927 by the movie industry to honor its artists and craftsmen. All categories of motion picture endeavor are honored, but the most significant are listed below.

BEST ACTOR
1950 José Ferrer *Cyrano de Bergerac*
1951 Humphrey Bogart *The African Queen*
1952 Gary Cooper *High Noon*
1953 William Holden *Stalag 17*
1954 Marlon Brando *On the Waterfront*
1955 Ernest Borgnine *Marty*
1956 Yul Brynner *The King and I*
1957 Alec Guinness *The Bridge on the River Kwai*
1958 David Niven *Separate Tables*
1959 Charlton Heston *Ben-Hur*

BEST ACTRESS
1950 Judy Holliday *Born Yesterday*
1951 Vivien Leigh *A Streetcar Named Desire*
1952 Shirley Booth *Come Back, Little Sheba*
1953 Audrey Hepburn *Roman Holiday*
1954 Grace Kelly *The Country Girl*
1955 Anna Magnani *The Rose Tattoo*
1956 Ingrid Bergman *Anastasia*
1957 Joanne Woodward *The Three Faces of Eve*
1958 Susan Hayward *I Want to Live!*
1959 Simone Signoret *Room at the Top*

BEST DIRECTOR
1950 Joseph L. Mankiewicz *All About Eve*
1951 George Stevens *A Place in the Sun*
1952 John Ford *The Quiet Man*
1953 Fred Zinnemann *From Here to Eternity*
1954 Elia Kazan *On the Waterfront*
1955 Delbert Mann *Marty*
1956 George Stevens *Giant*
1957 David Lean *The Bridge on the River Kwai*
1958 Vincente Minnelli *Gigi*
1959 William Wyler *Ben-Hur*

BEST PICTURE
1950 *All About Eve*
1951 *An American in Paris*
1952 *The Greatest Show on Earth*
1953 *From Here to Eternity*
1954 *On the Waterfront*
1955 *Marty*
1956 *Around the World in 80 Days*
1957 *The Bridge on the River Kwai*
1958 *Gigi*
1959 *Ben-Hur*

NOBEL PRIZES
The Nobel Prizes are an international award granted in the fields of literature, physics, chemistry, physiology or medicine, and peace. The first prizes were awarded in 1901 and funded by the money left in the will of the Swedish inventor Alfred Nobel (1833–1896), who gave the world dynamite.

PRIZES FOR LITERATURE
1950 Bertrand Russell (British) for philosophic writing
1951 Par Fabian Lagerkvist (Swedish) for fiction, particularly *Barabbas*
1952 François Mauriac (French) for fiction, essays and poetry
1953 Sir Winston Churchill (British) for essays, speeches and historical writings
1954 Ernest Hemingway (American) for fiction
1955 Halldor Laxness (Icelandic) for fiction
1956 Juan Ramon Jimenez (Spanish) for poetry
1957 Albert Camus (French) for fiction
1958 Boris Pasternak (Soviet) for fiction, especially *Dr Zhivago* (award declined).
1959 Salvatore Quasimodo (Italian) for lyric poetry

PRIZES FOR PEACE
1950 Ralph J. Bunche (American) for his work as UN mediator in Palestine in 1948 and 1949
1951 Leon Jouhaux (French) for work helping to organize national and international trade unions
1952 Albert Schweitzer (German-born) for humanitarian work in Africa (award delayed until 1953)
1953 George Marshall (American) for promoting peace through the European Recovery Program
1954 Office of the United Nations High Commissioner for Refugees for providing protection for millions of refugees and seeking permanent solutions to their problems (award delayed until 1955)
1955 *No awards*
1956 *No awards*
1957 Lester Pearson (Canadian) for organizing a UN force in Egypt
1958 Dominique Georges Pire (Belgian) for work in resettling displaced persons
1959 Lord Noel-Baker (British) for promoting peace and disarmament

PRIZES FOR PHYSICS
1950 Cecil Frank Powell (British) for the photographic method of studying atomic nuclei and discoveries concerning mesons
1951 Sir John Cockcroft (British) and Ernest Walton (Irish) for working on the transmutation of atomic nuclei by artificially accelerated atomic particles
1952 Felix Bloch and Edward Mills Purcell (American) for developing magnetic measurement methods for atomic nuclei
1953 Frits Zernike (Dutch) for inventing the phase contrast microscope for cancer research
1954 Max Born (German) for research in quantum mechanics and Walter Bothe (German) for discoveries made with the coincidence method
1955 Willis E. Lamb, Jr. (American) for discoveries on the structure of the hydrogen spectrum, and Polykarp Kusch (American) for determining the magnetic moment of the electron
1956 John Bardeen, Walter Brattain and William Schockley (American) for inventing the transistor
1957 Tsung Dao Lee and Chen Ning Yang (American) for disproving the law of conservation of parity
1958 Pavel Cherenkov, Ilya Frank and Igor Tamm (Soviet) for discovering and interpreting the Cherenkov effect in studying high-energy particles
1959 Emilio Segre and Owen Chamberlain (American) for work in demonstrating the existence of the antiproton

PRIZES FOR CHEMISTRY
1950 Otto Diels and Kurt Alder (German) for developing a method of synthesizing organic compounds of the diene group
1951 Edwin M. McMillan and Glenn T. Seaborg (American) for discovering plutonium and other elements
1952 Archer Martin and Richard Synge (British) for developing the partition chromatography process
1953 Hermann Staudinger (German) for discovering a way to synthesize fiber
1954 Linus Pauling (American) for work on the forces that hold matter together

ABOVE: Charles de Gaulle is elected first president of the Fifth Republic this year. He will remain in power until his resignation in 1969.

1955 Vincent Du Vigneaud (American) for discovering a process for making synthetic hormones
1956 Sir Cyril Hinshelwood (British) and Nikolai Semenov (Soviet) for work on chemical chain reactions
1957 Lord Todd (British) for work on the protein composition of cells
1958 Frederick Sanger (British) for discovering the structure of the insulin molecule
1959 Jaroslav Heyrovsky (Czech) for developing the polarographic method of analysis

PRIZES FOR PHYSIOLOGY OR MEDICINE
1950 Philip S. Hench, Edward C. Kendall (American) and Tadeus Reichstein (Swiss) for discoveries concerning cortisone and ACTH
1951 Max Theiler (South African-born) for developing the yellow fever vaccine known as 17-D
1952 Selman A. Waksman (American) for work in the discovery of streptomycin
1953 Fritz Albert Lipmann (American) and Hans Adolf Krebs (British) for discoveries in biosynthesis and metabolism
1954 John F. Enders, Thomas H. Weller and Frederick C. Robbins (American) for

discovering a simple method of growing polio virus in test tubes
1955 Hugo Theorell (Swedish) for discoveries on the nature and action of oxidation enzymes
1956 Andre F. Cournand, Dickinson W. Richards, Jr. (American) and Werner Forssmann (German) for using a catheter to chart the interior of the heart
1957 Daniel Bovet (Italian) for discovering antihistamines
1958 George Wells Beadle and Edward Lawrie Tatum (American) for work in biochemical genetics, and Joshua Lederberg (American) for studies of genetics in bacteria
1959 Severo Ochoa and Arthur Kornberg (American) for producing nucleic acid by artifical means

U.S. PRESIDENTS
1945–1953 President Harry S. Truman, *Democrat*
1949–1953 Vice President Alben W. Barkley
1953–1961 President Dwight David Eisenhower, *Republican*
1953–1961 Vice President Richard M. Nixon

SITES OF THE OLYMPIC GAMES
1952 SUMMER Helsinki, Finland
WINTER Oslo, Norway

1956 SUMMER Melbourne, Australia
WINTER Cortina, Italy

WORLD CUP FINAL MATCHES
YEAR	LOCATION
1950	**Rio de Janeiro**
Uruguay defeats Brazil 2-1	
1954	**Berne**
W. Germany defeats Hungary 3-2	
1958	**Stockholm**
Brazil defeats Sweden 5-2	

INDIANAPOLIS 500
1950 Johnnie Parsons
1951 Lee Wallard
1952 Troy Ruttman
1953 Bill Vukovich
1954 Bill Vukovich
1955 Bob Sweikert
1956 Pat Flaherty
1957 Sam Hanks
1958 Jimmy Bryan
1959 Rodger Ward

KENTUCKY DERBY
1950 Middleground
1951 Count Turf
1952 Hill Gail
1953 Dark Star
1954 Determine
1955 Swaps
1956 Needles
1957 Iron Liege
1958 Tim Tam
1959 Tomy Lee

NBA CHAMPIONS
1950 Minneapolis Lakers defeat Syracuse Nationals
1951 Rochester Royals defeat New York Knicks
1952 Minneapolis Lakers defeat New York Knicks
1953 Minneapolis Lakers defeat New York Knicks
1954 Minneapolis Lakers defeat Syracuse Nationals
1955 Syracuse Nationals defeat Fort Wayne Pistons
1956 Philadelphia Warriors defeat Fort Wayne Pistons
1957 Boston Celtics defeat St. Louis Hawks
1958 St. Louis Hawks defeat Boston Celtics
1959 Boston Celtics defeat Minneapolis Lakers

WIMBLEDON CHAMPIONS
1950 MEN Budge Patty
WOMEN Louise Brough
1951 MEN Dick Savitt
WOMEN Doris Hart
1952 MEN Frank Sedgman
WOMEN Maureen Connolly
1953 MEN Vic Seixas
WOMEN Maureen Connolly
1954 MEN Jaroslav Drobny
WOMEN Maureen Connolly
1955 MEN Tony Trabert
WOMEN Louise Brough
1956 MEN Lew Hoad
WOMEN Shirley Fry
1957 MEN Lew Hoad
WOMEN Althea Gibson
1958 MEN Ashley Cooper
WOMEN Althea Gibson
1959 MEN Alex Olmedo
WOMEN Maria Bueno

WORLD SERIES CHAMPIONS
1950 New York Yankees defeat Philadelphia Athletics
1951 New York Yankees defeat New York Giants
1952 New York Yankees defeat Brooklyn Dodgers
1953 New York Yankees defeat Brooklyn Dodgers
1954 New York Giants defeat Cleveland Indians
1955 Brooklyn Dodgers defeat New York Yankees
1956 New York Yankees defeat Brooklyn Dodgers
1957 Milwaukee Braves defeat New York Yankees
1958 New York Yankees defeat Milwaukee Braves
1959 Los Angeles Dodgers defeat Chicago White Sox